MW01194943

KNOCKED *DOWN,* SET STRAIGHT

FACE IT, SPEAK IT, FORGIVE IT, RELEASE IT.

LYNITA MITCHELL- BLACKWELL

Knocked Down, Set Straight: *Face It. Speak It. Forgive It. Release It.*
Published by Leading Through Living Community LLC

Copyright 2019 by Lynita Mitchell-Blackwell

ISBN 978-1-949266-10-8 Hardback
ISBN 978-1-949266-09-2 Paperback
ISBN 978-1-949266-11-5 E-book
ISBN 978-1-949266-12-2 Audiobook

Edited by Dorna Francine

For information:
Leading Through Living Community LLC
www.LeadingThroughLiving.com

CONTENTS

DEDICATION

THIS BOOK IS DEDICATED TO EVERY person who works to build a winning team, relationship, or organization, knowing that aspiration begins with Self.

If you thought your mistakes were messes to be cleaned up, know that they were actually re-takes of scenes in your life, as the word indicates – mis-take.

Trust the process. The re-take will be *so* worth it!

FOREWORD

WHEN I FIRST MET LYNITA, I WAS THE managing editor of a magazine. We met to discuss her desire to become a contributing writer and connected instantly. We came to find out we had so much in common. Lynita and I were both from the same hometown, were attorneys, and seemed to have some of the same professional goals- not to mention we were also moms and wives.

Following our meeting, we agreed she would be an excellent fit for the magazine. Over the next year, Lynita wrote numerous articles and became a top contributor. It does not surprise me at all that she has now created a media empire consisting of award-winning magazine publications and has authored numerous life-changing books.

Have you ever known someone that can make you reflect, improve, and take action after being with them for any amount of time? That is Lynita. She is like that in real-life encounters, as well as through her writing. She is a gifted writer who can tell a story as effectively with a pen as she can orally. Impacting lives through her writing is precisely what Lynita does in this book. Through her wit and knack for captivating an audience, she has created a mirror for the reader to examine himself or herself.

Over the years that I have known Lynita, I have come to learn that she genuinely cares about people becoming the best versions of themselves. She is passionate about ensuring that everyone she meets knows they are special and that they have a gift to contribute to the world. Lynita conveys her brilliance, faith and humor to the reader in this essential book.

The notion of an aggregate intelligence quotient will become apart of the way you see situations, other people and yourself. Prepare to be challenged by using not just your academic intelligence but also your spiritual and emotional intelligence. Her anecdotes illustrate her points and are completely relatable. Replete with Godly and natural principles, this book is sure to make every reader stronger and more resilient.

What you get in this book is what Lynita's friends get in real life. Candor and wisdom are present in every interaction, and she is giving that gift to the readers. I call it a gift because with the prevalence of social media, so many people are pressured to put forth an image of perfection. It is refreshing to hear stories of humanness— and *Knocked Down Set Straight* provides just that.

Prepare to be inspired, uplifted and to increase your

AQ! When you are having one of those days, you know those days when you may be feeling less than- pick up this book, choose a chapter and I guarantee that you will find the motivation to continue.

I decree that after you read this book, you will never be knocked down and stay down again. You will come to learn that there are lessons on the way down that help you to stand stronger!

Careshia Moore, Esq.
President & CEO
Usher's New Look
www.ushersnewlook.org

INTRODUCTION

MY PARENTS ALWAYS TOLD ME I WAS A smart child. I did well in school, so my cognitive intelligence (or intellectual quotient – IQ) was deemed to be high. As I grew older, I noticed that my successes came more from interacting well with people, getting a good sense of who they were and how I related to them. Thus, I began to work steadily to improve my emotional intelligence (or EQ). And then I began to desire a deep and more meaningful connection to the Great I Am, one that was beyond the restricted parent-child type relationship where I ask for something and half-way expect to hear 'no'. And so, I delved into the world of spiritual intelligence (or SQ).

In meeting new people who share their view of love and loss freely, traveling the world experiencing new things, learning to appreciate small things such as the smell of fresh lemons as dawn breaks across my neighborhood – these things drew me to a startling insight: All of these quotients, IQ, EQ, and SQ combine to an intelligence that resides in all of us, one I term the Aggregate Intelligence

Quotient (or AQ). AQ recognizes that there is a fourth state in human evolution that is the composite of mind, body, and soul. This joint state of being has its own way of navigating the world and imparts knowledge, wisdom, and love in its own way to each person. One of those ways is the processing of pain. Why pain?

Pain is a useful tool. We don't like to admit it, but some of the most impactful lessons in life have come to us through pain.

I've had a lot of time to consider why pain is such a great teacher. Pain halts us in our tracks and gives us time to reconsider our course. Pain forces us to acknowledge that which we would continue to ignore forever if left to our own devices. Pain pushes us through barriers of preconceived limitations of what we thought we could endure. Pain removes perceived obstacles to what's holding us back from our destiny. Pain corrects us when we are out of order. Pain brings us appreciation of what we have – and don't have.

If we refuse to allow bitterness and self-pity to swallow us whole, pain can be a transformative agent. There is beauty in pain. Pain can lead to beauty. There is knowledge in pain. Pain can lead to knowledge. There is wisdom in pain. Pain can lead to wisdom. But how? How do we embrace the very thing we've been taught to run from since childhood?

I remember the following warnings growing up, usually said in a harsh voice when I was being disobedient:

"A hard head makes for a soft behind."

But once you learned the lesson for yourself, you never had to be taught again . . . and sometimes you were driven to be creative to ensure the lesson never extended to others. Your AQ began to work.

"This is a tree you don't want to climb."

Your AQ began to work, pushing you to face the challenge (usually a person!), and you either got knocked out and learned to overcome in a different way, or you won and learned you could climb a bigger tree.

"Pride cometh before destruction."

Your AQ allowed you to do the work that brought forth that pride and helped you to get through the destruction it wrought. And after the destruction, you realized there was a chance to survey the land and rebuild something better and stronger.

Pain is a tool, and just like any tool, it can be used for both good and bad. And just like any tool, the most effective use comes from mastery. Mastering the use of a tool requires observation, study, and practice.

Observation is easy. Pain is a part of life, so we have plenty of opportunities to see pain and its effects in action. Funerals, not-so-random shootings, firings, losses in competitive sports, financial crises, and mental and physical illnesses provide so many chances to see pain at its most acute. But once we observe, we must then turn our attention to study.

Dictionary.com defines "study" as "the devotion of time and attention to acquiring knowledge on an academic subject, especially by means of books." But there is also a secondary definition: "A detailed investigation and analysis of a subject or situation". It's this second definition that we need to employ in our desire to transform pain into a useful and effective tool for our benefit.

We must investigate, analyze, scrutinize, and get to the very core of why we are in pain before real change can come. But sometimes that means leaving a situation as it is and allowing the pain to continue to resonate through our being before action may be taken, i.e., allowing our AQ to fully take it in. Think about it, when a detective surveys a crime scene, she secures the perimeter and ensures nothing is disturbed. This is to ensure the room may be thoroughly studied – or analyzed – so she may figure out what happened there. Pain in our lives must be scrutinized in the same way. We must review the circumstances that occurred and honestly assess what happened and why. We learn from pain. We learn what works and what doesn't. Once we obtain this knowledge, we may now make pain our tool and use it for our benefit.

And benefits many times translate to prosperity. Prosperous physical health, emotional wellbeing, mental acuity, and spiritual strength are all components of a high AQ.

People want to be with winners, those whose lives are prosperous and blessed. If you want people to gravitate towards you, your business, and the causes you care about, they must feel valued, cared about, and part of the winner's circle. Embrace them. Rope them in. Show them all the good and bad that went into you becoming you. Help them to strengthen and grow their AQ's by seeing past the terms "good" and "bad" and enjoy – be in real joy – the state of "is".

Pain is more than a tool of punishment sent from On High to smite the enemy. Pain is a tool to be used to move us forward, but for that to happen, we must embrace it. All of it - the Aggregate Intelligence.

Embrace the pain and watch the blessings rain.

Embrace the pain and watch the blessings reign.

CHAPTER 1

MOVE OUT OF THE DUMP. RENEW YOUR MIND AND STOP THRIVING IN FOOLISHNESS

MAGGOTS ARE DISGUSTING. THEY ONLY come up when there is something rotten going on. Whether it is some wound or some fruit or rotting flesh, you are going to find a maggot. But did you know that there was a time when maggots were used for medicinal purposes? Physicians would set the maggots upon dead rotting flesh to remove it from the clean thriving flesh. Maggots do not eat live flesh so when they stopped eating, the Healer or Medicine Man removed them from the wound. Once removed, the doctor cleaned and bandaged the wound. Prior to the maggots doing their work, if the doctor had tried to clean and wrap the injury, it would have simply become worse and the person would have lost a limb and possibly life as well.

1

There are certain people in the world who really do thrive in mess. They like being stressed out, they like being a part of drama, and they like being the people who instigate all kinds of confusion. These are people I like to call Those Who Thrive on Foolishness. Foolish behavior is akin to stupid behavior. You are not stupid, nor were you born foolish. And yet, we all put on the Clown costume and star in the Fool Circus from time to time.

There was a time when Those Who Thrive on Foolishness disgusted me. I would see them laughing in the background as they watched events unfold based on some lie they told or some mean thing they said. Now I look at those people as sad people. I also look at those people as necessary evils. Before you get angry and think, "What the heck is Lynita talking about?!" let me take you through it.

Those Who Thrive on Foolishness are maggots because at the end of the day they need to attach to rotten flesh in order to thrive. If they are ignored, if they are disregarded, if they are sat down as soon as they start to work, there is no flesh for them to eat and they die. People like that have to have others who are willing to engage with them. So, if a person is thriving in foolishness that means that **there is something or someone feeding them.** There is an environment in which they are thriving, that is ripe with rotting pestilent nasty garbage. So if you see someone thriving in foolishness, if you see their lies taking root, if you see their mean-spiritedness taking hold and causing confusion, that means that there is an environment conducive to that negative breeding that existed *prior to them coming to be* that needs to be changed.

Yep, I can here you swearing in tongues. How dare I tell you that the maggot came into your life, into your home, into your job, into your mind because there was a welcoming environment for it? Who do I think I am to tell you that all your prayers, meditation, forgiveness, and sacrifice won't ward off stupidity? Did I just get in your face and tell you that your best intentions can still pave the path to hell? Yes, I did. I know what attracts maggots and what repels maggots and all your good works don't mean a thing. How do I know? Because I was a maggot.

I used to like listening to gossip (just between us girls), sharing gossip (don't tell anyone I told you this), evaluating the veracity of the gossip (take this with a grain of salt), bridging the gaps in gossip (she didn't say this, but I know for a fact that), and repacking gossip (I heard it directly from). And it never crossed my mind as a young woman the hard time I was creating for myself or for the people with whom I was sharing this stuff. Note that I said "sharing". A gossiper needs someone to gossip to — someone has to listen, someone has to share, someone has to "be in on it" for the mess to stick. So, it is not that I shoulder all the blame myself; rather, I realize that there was a reason I felt comfortable talking in such a way to those particular people.

"Hurt people hurt people" is the old saying. But what happens when you don't realize that you are hurt? What happens when you don't understand that *you* are the maggot? How do you evaluate yourself and make the changes necessary to get out of larva mode?

1. BE QUIET AND LISTEN.

Who is talking to you?

What are they saying?

How does it make you feel?

Where does what is being said fit into your prosperous mind life?

When will you see the benefit of what is being shared?

If you cannot answer all of the above in a positive, affirmative manner, then beloved, you are in larva mode – living in filth.

If people feel comfortable coming to you with mess, you have attracted it. If they know you, and they feel comfortable coming to you with mess, it is because they believe you will be comfortable with it. If those people don't even try to bridge the gap between what they are saying and how and when it will prosper and benefit you, then you have not displayed the requisite demeanor to convey that your mind is not a dump.

Tough to hear, but as the Good Book says, "the truth shall set you free". So, let's get free.

There is value in those people, the people who parade as maggots, because it shows that there is something wrong that needs to be addressed. Some relationship that needs to be repaired. A friendship that should have never been. A relationship between a man and a woman that needs Jesus. There is something that needs to be addressed, cleansed, set straight and put under God's holy and anointed care.

2. SPEAK LIFE.

"The power of life and death are in the tongue." Every day is not a box of chocolates, bad things happen and they require us to take action – which includes talking about those things. But is the talking moving things forward? Is talking about the thing airing out the stale air? Is the discussion worthy of our energy and attention? Are we engaging in dialogue for the edification of our minds, hearts, souls, communities, homes, relationships? Is it impacting, in a positive manner, our wellbeing or the wellbeing of others?

If we cannot answer these questions in the affirmative, then we must elevate – or as the singer Ciara sings so eloquently, it's time to "Level Up".

Just by doing these two things have I moved out of the dump. And because I know what it was like to live there, to feel the mistrustful gazes and to hear the measured words that all who live in the dump experience at some point, it is my hope that you can use these simple steps to get out and stay out of that place.

Now, I do not begrudge that experience. I believe it has made me more compassionate and empathetic, even when such could be viewed as insanely unsafe to others. My mother and I were on the way home from a party one evening and we came across a fruit stand on the side of the road. In the South the fruit stands have the best produce you have ever tasted. When we pulled up, the trailer that was attached to the fruit stand had a Confederate Battle Flag on it. That flag represents heritage to some, and blatant oppression and racism to me. However, as I was leaving that stand, I did not feel anger or resentment toward that flag or the people who had it on their car, even though it signifies to *me* the horrors that my ancestors overcame so that I could be. What came to my mind and flowed through my heart was compassion because I've learned to ask the question:

"Where and when am I meeting you in your story?"

Life is like a TV show that you pick up in the middle. We meet people and want to judge them at the exact moment we meet, but that is not realistic at all. Just like every person has a back story, so too, do we, have a front story and a middle story. At all times we are products of what has happened before, what is happening now, and what is about to happen. We know this intellectually, but emotionally, we judge other people as if who they are at this moment has nothing to do with what happened before or what's happening around them right now.

People who spew hate and divisiveness are unhappy and scared. A lot of them don't know from where their next meal is coming. Many of them are working jobs just to see all that money going to pay bills that never end. It's one of those things that can break your heart.

It is easier to believe that the source of one's troubles is someone else. When we have someone to blame, we can give our responsibility for our happiness and wellbeing to someone we can point the finger at when things do not go our way. But the truth is that we have all made choices that led to us being where we are in our lives. I'm not talking about the choice to be born poor, or the choice to be abused, or the choice to attend a dangerous school, or the choice to be drafted into war. I'm talking about the choice to pay a bill on time or skip it and move somewhere else to start again and pay that bill later. The choice to open a book and learn something new about something you think you know. The opportunity to see life through someone else's eyes and feel what they feel. The choice to be truly united as "one nation, under God, indivisible, with liberty and justice for all".

But for that to happen, we must aspire to operate at

a level of empathy that up to this point has only been embraced by the masters and great gurus.

You are a master. You are a guru. You were made in God's image. You are a son and daughter of the Most High. Divine Mind crafted you in greatness and love. Both course through your veins, surging with a strength that allows you to overcome and forgive the unimaginable. A maggot *thrives* in foolishness. Small minded, misguided people do well in the dump. How much MORE will you achieve as a master in the universe? How much greater will you be as a guru in love with man- and woman-kind? Embrace your wonder and wow, your all-encompassing awesomesauceness and thrive in excellence!

Blessings from the Lessons

1. Everything in your life has value - the good and bad. If bad is there, examine it, learn from it, then take steps to remove it.

2. You are ultimately responsible for your own wellbeing, prosperity, and spiritual actualization. You were born with the requisite knowledge and skills to bring these things into divine order. Act now to make it happen. Doing so honors the past lessons and embraces ownership of and ushers in future blessings.

CHAPTER 2

VALUE IN THE FILTER: MULTIPLE ATTITUDINAL DISPLAY DISORDER AKA NASTY GIRL

IN ORDER FOR YOU TO BREAK OUT, YOU have to be willing to be broken down.

My freshman year in high school was unremarkable. I was a normal awkward teen girl trying to manage a monster load of work and not look like a big nerd doing it (I failed).

But one day I decided that I didn't want to just exist – I wanted my life to mean something. I wish I could tell you that my decision was the result of some awe-inspiring encounter or some profound book passage, but nope, that's just not true. It happened one day as I was walking through our Hall of Fame.

The Hall of Fame was filled with high school seniors who were outstanding graduates. They were popular, smart, and most of them were good-looking. I remember stopping dead in my tracks and looking up at those pictures one day and saying to myself, "One day, I am going to be on that wall." I then turned to walk away, and never thought about being on that wall again.

The next four years were transformative in every way – physically, mentally, emotionally, and spiritually. I grew taller and got active, so my "baby-fat" finally gave way. I dug into my course work and put aside osmosis as my primary study tool. I volunteered as a tutor and got involved in both school and community groups, gaining a great appreciation as to what real economic struggle was (no Virginia, getting "only" $20 a week in allowance does not qualify). And I joined the band. That was one of the most wonderful times in my life. And it almost broke me in half.

I was a good kid, but I had multiple attitudinal display disorder. Sometimes, I was really cool. Other times . . . well . . . not so much. It wasn't that I was disrespectful or rude. It was that I didn't use the filter the good Lord gives all of us to determine whether something REALLY needs to be said.

One day it all came to a head and I learned The Value of the Filter.

My band director was having a particularly hard day. We all were. It was unbearably hot that summer, so band camp was broken into two parts – morning and afternoon.

We did most of the outside work in the morning while it was hot. We did the specialized routines and other work inside in the afternoon while it was hot as hell.

One of the hot-as-hell afternoons found us all in bad tempers. I had gotten into a spat with one of the other kids, and my friends took my side and her friends took her side, and all of our backsides were sent to the band director's office. He was annoyed. That should have been the first sign that I should have just let him rant and rave, been quiet, and leave to fight another day.

But no.

During the ranting and raving, my band director said something that wasn't true. (Just so you know how unimportant it was, I can't even remember what he said.) I called him on it. I quoted it back to him verbatim.

Lord. Have. Mercy.

My band director went off. He really lost his mind. It was so bad, the assistant band director, who was a mild-mannered man, slowly backed out of the room and left. He didn't come back.

As things go when we lose control, the attack got personal. He started calling me names. And then the worst happened. He said, "You're just a nasty little girl. Just horrible."

No one had ever spoken to me like that before. It hurt me so bad, I broke down crying. As I ran out of his office, I remembered saying, "I want to go home, I want to go home!" I made it as far as the stairs before my legs just wouldn't support me anymore and I collapsed . . . right into the warm embrace of a fellow band member I'd never met before.

She was so sweet and she didn't even speak English. She was a recent immigrant who'd just come to our school. She held me and rocked me like a little child, whispering some mix of Spanglish to comfort me. When I got myself together, I thanked her and went back to the band room to gather my things. My friends were relieved to see me. They didn't know where I'd taken off to once I ran out. I told them what happened and I told them I wasn't coming back.

I rode the city bus home alone and had a lot of time to think. I was hurt, angry, and ready to do damage. But I also had the presence of mind to know that I had a part to play in what happened in that office.

My parents raised me to be respectful and mannerable. They taught me that every battle doesn't have to be fought today, fought by me, and sometimes, not at all. The sequence of events that led to that horrendous tongue lashing was a battle I didn't need to fight AT ALL. Yes, there was an injustice (I do remember that part), but it wasn't worth the incredible take down of my self-confidence.

But I learned from it.

1. LIVE TO FIGHT ANOTHER DAY.

I learned the value of silence. My silence does NOT mean consent or agreement. It means that I will deal with a situation in my own time and in my own way. I also learned the value of walking away. Allowing cooler heads to prevail can avoid saying things that cannot be unsaid and deeply wounding people I care about.

2. REMEMBER THE ULTIMATE BATTLE; DO NOT GET DISTRACTED BY SKIRMISHES.

I learned the value of working through my own challenges, without involving those I cared about, until I had a clear path to MY end game. I didn't tell my parents about that episode until I was in my thirties, and it was only when one of them told me they'd run into my old band director and he asked about me. Even in my bruised emotional state, I knew if I told my parents that this man had called their precious child a "nasty girl", they would not rest until he had been reduced to professional ashes. As mad as I was at him, I knew that he had "something coming", but he didn't deserve that.

And my end game was that I wanted to stay in the band. I went back after I had cooled my jets a couple of days later and my band director looked relieved to see me.

He didn't say anything, and neither did I. I just took my position and fell in line.

3. CIRCLE BACK AND ADDRESS ISSUES AT THE TIME AND PLACE OF YOUR CHOOSING.

I also learned that not talking about things and pretending things are fine do not lead to healing or resolution. My band director and I never really patched it up. There was always uneasiness between us, even after I graduated. So, I learned the value of not just clearing the slate but cleaning it, too.

In coming back to the band, I had experiences that nurtured me, challenged me, matured me, and I was mentored and loved and supported by amazing people – both adults and students. And although I was involved in other activities and earned high scholastic honors and achievements, it was those transformative experiences in band that allowed me to be inducted into my high school's Hall of Fame.

Blessings from the Lessons

1. Embrace the value in the filter. Does "that" need to be said, right now, and by you? Can you let this

"ride" - is it better to live and fight AND WIN another day?

2. What part did you play in The Great Drama of the harm and what should you have done differently (there is always something)? Is there something you can (or should) do right now to rectify things?

3. Silence is not consent. Allow cooler heads to prevail. Visualize the clear path to your end game - how you want things to end.

4. What is the consequence of next steps to you and the other person? How do you get what you want out of this situation?

CHAPTER 3

CLAIM THE HEART & LOYALTY OF YOUR PEOPLE TO STOP "THE GAME AND THE LIES"

MY GRANDMOTHER TAUGHT ME A valuable lesson years ago based on an exchange she had with my older cousin. My cousin decided one Sunday morning that she wanted to wear pants to church. It wasn't just that she wanted to wear pants, it was the entire outfit as a whole. The shirt was a black and white vertical striped number that had seen better days and hung loosely off her tall, nicely built frame. And the pants...O. M. G. The pants. The pants at one time were black, but at this point in history were faded kinda like charcoal as you're preparing for a good barbeque. They were wrinkled and looked like they'd been worn at least thrice before.

Now, to give you some context, my cousin put on this getup to get on my grandmother's nerves. Church was and is a BIG deal in my family. We go to church wearing our best, and when I was growing up, girls did not wear pants to church – not even pantsuits. Added to that, my grandmother was a First Lady, i.e., my grandfather was THE pastor! So, you KNOW my grandmother was fly EVERY Sunday! For my teenage cousin to walk into my grandmother's room and announce that she was dressed and ready to go wearing that train-wreck of an outfit was shocking, stunning, incredibly stupid, and outrageous all rolled up into a nice no-the-hell-she-didn't bun. AND (like you need more, right?!) she said the reason she was wearing the outfit was because she hadn't brought anything else to wear!

My younger cousins and I all stood still waiting to see what would happen. We all just KNEW our older cousin was about to get the beat-down for real! I watched my grandmother take in the outfit, her eyes roving up and down my cousin's statuesque physique hidden by this ugly tent. We needn't have worried. We'd forgotten that our grandmother had lived more than four times as long as we and had seen all the games and lies.

My grandmother was not going to allow her joy, i.e., her Jesus, to be stolen from her on Sunday morning - no emotional hijacking here! Not by burned bacon ("Eat it anyway, it'll scrape your intestines!"), poorly conceived feigned illness ("Don't feel good, it's okay, you just won't play the rest of the week so you'll be better in time for next

Sunday."), and certainly not by my not-so-slick cousin who just wanted to get on her nerves.

My grandmother simply looked at my cousin and said, "You ain't sittin' next to me wearing britches," calmly turned away and went about her business.

An adult cousin saw the exchange and went in search of something more appropriate for my teenage cousin to wear. But it wasn't necessary because whatdaya know? When my teenage cousin saw that my grandmother was not going to engage with her, was not going to demand she change, and was not going to allow her to sit anywhere NEAR her in the church . . . she all of a sudden "found" the outfit her mom had sent with her to wear!

So . . . what does this have to do with pain? **Everything!** People lie in fear, they lie in anger, and sometimes they lie to test you. My cousin was testing my grandmother, seeing how far she could go, and my grandmother showed her the line. My grandmother refused to engage AND made it clear that her approval and support were a no-go as long as my cousin did not conform to the norm.

When people are close, they tend to take support and approval for granted. When the support and approval are removed, there is a void left in their place. And if that void is not filled with someone else's support and approval, people refer back to the original source.

Have you ever worked so hard on something that wasn't even your idea, sacrificed your time, spent your money, used your personal and professional credibility to get others behind it, only for it to flop big? And all because people who SHOULD have been supporting it wanted to play stupid games and tell bold-faced lies.

Well, if not, keep living – it'll come!

One of the things I've learned about running multiple businesses is that your business is only as good as the STATE of MIND of the people working with you. If you have a person's heart, you have their loyalty. They will literally kick the butt of anybody who talks about you – no matter your flaws, shortcomings, and downright insanity. So, I work hard to ensure that the people in my organization are working my dream AND their dreams at all times. It creates a rub sometimes, but it's worth it because I always get the benefit of the doubt when things go haywire. If there is a choice between believing me and backing me when outsiders say and do things to undermine my credibility, I simply refer my folks back to the evidence of my support of their dreams. My real support, i.e., my time, talent, and treasure. Very few times has the outsider been able to trump my past and current service.

So fast forward to my life as a publisher. Two of our stars came to me and said, "We want to start a plus-size calendar." Ummmmm, okay. We'd never done a calendar, they'd never done a calendar, but hey, let's jump off the ledge! And we did. Our stars had the model call, negotiated the contracts with the photographers and make-up artists and designers, coordinated the photo-shoots, organized the "calendar girls and guys", and selected monthly inspirations. The graphic designer pulled it all together, ordered them from one of our staple companies, and viola, we had a calendar! And our stars were happy.

We released the calendar at our annual magazine awards program to great acclaim. People were so supportive of the mission which was to confront and combat body-shaming. My stars' friends were gung-ho about buying tons of copies to send to their friends all over the world. My stars were riding high! Me too – we were going to recoup our expenses and make a profit! Wooohooo!

But that's not how it happened.

We sold 10 copies of the calendar. I didn't stutter. T-E-N. And it was a slllloooowwww sell over the first four months. I couldn't believe it. And my stars DIDN'T believe it. At first, they thought I was holding out on them. But God had blessed me with the insight to set up a separate payment system to process the calendar sales from the magazine purchases. So, when the following convoluted question came, I was ready:

"I know you're always looking out for us and value our hard work and only want us to be happy and put a lot of time and money into this project and you didn't really want to do it and you had to get expedited shipping because we turned everything in late and we put in a lot of money to

traveling to the sites and hosting the model call and we really do appreciate you and people have purchased so many copies and we thought we'd see more traffic but understand you're really busy and well when will we get paid?"

It was almost as painful writing that as it was listening to it. Almost.

I was annoyed that my stars would take the word (or even words) of buffoons who were clearly lying about buying calendars. But I knew that I would need to show the evidence of my past and current loyalty so they would demand the same of these outsiders…and I could once again get my stars focused back on my dream. So I laid it down.

1. ESTABLISH SYSTEMS OF ACCOUNTABILITY (I.E., SHOW 'EM BETTER THAN YOU CAN TELL 'EM).

I sent my team members the system report, that had the date, time, and range printed on the bottom so they'd have independent, verifiable evidence of sales. And of course, there were none (10 is closer to zero than 1,000, so for the sake of this illustration and in light of the expense of producing the calendar, I am saying none.)

2. DEMAND EXTERNAL VERIFICATION AND FEEDBACK.

I then told them to go back to each person who said they'd purchased a calendar and ask them to do the following: Hold the calendar next to their faces, take a selfie, and post it to social media. If that happened one time, my name is Ted.

3. EVALUATE AND MOVE ON.

My stars were horrified and embarrassed and angry . . . and scared. They were scared that I would remove my approval and support based on this misread of the tea leaves. Thankfully, I'm not that shallow.

I was annoyed that my stars had not trusted me, annoyed that they tested me and tried me. But just as my grandmother had done so many years before in a similar situation, I showed my stars where the line was and how to get back across it. When my stars realized they'd been played and came back to inform me of the result of the selfie test, I forgave and took them back across the line. With me. They'd put on their good church clothes, and now they could sit next to me, minus the britches.

Blessings from the Lessons

1. We dream, then manifest, and it all starts in the mind. What is your state of mind? Is it fertile ground in which a seed may take root and grow?

2. People are going to test you, so be ready and confident with your answer. Establish systems so you may serve your answer strong and good - think Serena Williams on her best day at Wimbledon!

3. Your attention is currency, so spend it on things that matter. Investing in foolishness is a guaranteed negative ROI.

CHAPTER 4

BE THE CALVARY YOU SEEK BECAUSE YOU ARE THE MAGIC BULLET.

"The cavalry isn't coming. I <u>was</u> the cavalry."
Chris Gardner

"<u>You</u> are the cavalry." Lisa Nichols

"Oh, Sugar Honey Iced Tea - I need a cavalry?!" Lynita Mitchell-Blackwell

NEWSFLASH: IN TODAY'S EDITION OF "Lynita's Life," a big purpose was laid on her life by the Father Almighty. The ultimate goal was and is to strike the match that sets fires in the souls of others to walk successfully in their gifts. Playing with matches can be deadly. The fire burns both ways. Lynita does not always remember that. Proceed with caution.

If only our lives came with actual newsflashes and words of caution. But alas, that is not the case. However, our lives do come with directions for use. And it's up to us to follow them or not.

Years ago, I attended a conference to expand my speaking, publishing, and public relations skills. I firmly believe in lifelong learning, continual and consistent training, and forever self and personal development (it's the FAMU SBIan in me!). In staying sharp, I'm able to assist my own clients to do the same. So, each year I drop a pretty penny on courses to expand my heart, mind, and soul. This conference did all that and then some, just not in the way I imagined.

We were tasked with doing a partner exercise based on several live simulations. We were not to coach. We were NOT to coach. WE WERE NOT TO COACH. Did I mention we weren't supposed to coach?

But your friend Lynita coached. I thought I was helping, and I wound up wounding my partner.

My partner with her beautifully kind eyes and warm smile and shining ebony skin. My partner who was looking to sharpen her skills and take back knowledge to her tribe. My partner who is a sister in the struggle with me. I hurt my partner because I would not follow instructions.

In my mind, this wonderful woman just needed to make this tiny little itsy bitsy correction to her pitch and then all would be perfect according to the instructions.

THEN she'd be able to go out and win countless clients and supporters to her tribe. I give her credit. She was firm yet kind in resisting me. I wanted to light the match. I wanted to set the fire. But just because you have matches doesn't mean they should be used.

There's no need for a fire in the summer.

There's no need for an additional fire in a single room.

And only a crazy person lights a fire in a dry forest with no flame retardant.

And yet that's exactly what I did. All of those things.

The seminar was to strengthen and train us in doing something we COULD do to get more clients, not that we HAD to do to get any clients. It was summer and I was trying to light a fire.

The seminar was to strengthen and undergird us in a safe, nurturing environment where we would be loved and supported, not to turn us into mini-me's who fell victim to "the process". There was one room and I was trying to light a second fire in it.

The seminar was to strengthen and push us to try something different and uncomfortable WHEN WE WERE READY TO TRY IT, not that we had to do it TODAY. I tried to light a fire in a dry forest with no flame retardant. I was crazy and downright mad.

As noble as my reasoning was – that my sister-friend had spent all this money to learn a new system and needed a little boost to get it "right" so she'd get the cluck for her buck – it was wrong. As well-meaning as my fortitude to keep trying to get her to "give it the old college try", it was wrong. The road to hell is paved with good intentions.

In realizing my mistake, I dove into the question that most of us hate, but boosts our EQ (and therefore strengthens our overall AQ): **Why?** Why did I do that? Why did I disregard the instructions? Why did I push so hard? What was so important that I just HAD to strike the match?

1. WITH THE EXCEPTION OF SMALL CHILDREN AND CERTAIN ADULTS, PEOPLE ARE CAPABLE OF SAVING THEMSELVES.

I wanted to be my friend's cavalry. I wanted to save her. But SHE DIDN'T NEED SAVING. She didn't need saving. Not by me. Not by any person. SHE was her shero. Her.

Some of us are waiting for some force outside ourselves to come and save us. Some of us are looking for some magic recipe that is going to do it all for us. There is no external force that's going to get things done for you. You've got to do it for yourself. I know that sounds strange and contradicts my faith background but go with me for a moment.

God doesn't push His will on anyone. He waits for us to open our hearts and let Him in. Free will. We have a choice to do or not to do. To act or not to act. To rush in and try to save the day or to allow others the chance to do for themselves and come in IF THEY REQUEST assistance.

2. THE STRUGGLE IS REAL, AND IT IS NECESSARY - GO THROUGH IT.

There is no success worth having that doesn't require effort, money, skill, and connections. However, it all begins within. YOU are the miracle. You are your own miracle! You are everything that you have been looking for all of your life.

In forgetting the above lesson, I harmed my sister-friend. I deeply regret that wound I unintentionally yet clumsily inflicted, and it'll be a long time before I forget that lesson.

3. DECIDE WHERE YOU WANT YOUR SAFE PLACE TO BE.

I also learned the lesson of ARE. There are no good people or bad people in the world, only people. At each moment we decide who we want to be. We do not come into this world Good or Bad. We come in as a person, made in Divine Mind's image. At any time we can be who we want to BE. So, at your core you ARE. You decide what comes after ARE - or not. You decide to be good, decide to be bad, decide to be amazing, or decide to be ordinary. You decide every moment on the state of your ARE.

And I chose to be in the state of ARE amazing! At least until the next time I hear the word, "Charge!".

Blessings from the Lessons

1. You are not here to save anyone except yourself. It's a full-time job, so commit to it fully.
2. The purpose of a match is to set a fire. Handle with care.
3. Asking "why?" after you've hurt someone will cause discomfort - do it anyway. Embrace the lesson and the blessing together.

CHAPTER 5

SAY SOMETHING, THE RIGHT THING, THAT ENCOMPASSES EVERYTHING

I'VE STRUGGLED MOST OF MY LIFE WITH timing. I've gotten better at it as I've gotten older, but I take more time than most people to consider what to say and when. Although I always knew what I meant when I said something, sometimes others aren't so clear. (Amazing, since I'm in the communications business!)

Years ago, I was a guest in my former employer's skybox during a football game, laughing and talking with my colleagues. I thought things were going really well. We talked about the game, the food, and plans for the remaining hours of the weekend. There were about 12 of us, and everyone chimed in to share their opinions on everything, trading stories and telling jokes. Then one of the managers turned to me and asked, "Lynita, are you the baby of your family?"

I was naive and unsuspecting, and responded with cheer, "No, I'm the third child. Why?" I asked the question, totally not understanding that she was preparing to make me a punchline.

And she gut-punched me with, "Wow, I can't believe that. You always have something to say." Everyone laughed, and I smiled uncertainly. Actually, it wasn't without certainty – I knew she was making fun of me, I just didn't understand why. So, I swallowed my comeback, excused myself to go to the ladies' room, and gathered my composure. I remember staring at the mirror for a long time, wondering how many more of those blows I'd have to take in my quest to climb the corporate ladder. (Sadly, there were many more to come, and this was comparatively gentle to some of the things that did.)

I'd love to tell you that I shook off what my former manager said, and pushed forward with being the vivacious, charismatic, brilliantly bold person I strive to be today . . . but that'd be a lie, and we're cool, so I won't lie to you. I internalized what my manager said and allowed it to stifle my voice for years in situations that could have really used my energy to make the world a better place.

I don't say that with any arrogance. Rather, it's an acknowledgement that there were times that God placed me in the room because I had the knowledge, credentials, education, and experience to speak up and make a difference . . . and I didn't. I allowed the half-drunk ramblings of a wounded, overworked, stressed-out person from my early 20's to ring in my head like a bell in a tower.

And what's so crazy is that I didn't realize it until I received a text from my husband's old secretary calling me out about it. Sweetly, gently, and with all the love I imagine Christ Himself would have infused in the text, but still, she called me to the carpet.

A few days prior to receiving The Text, our missionary society had a great discussion on prison reform. It was a small group of about 12 people (what is it about the number 12?), and we talked about individuals and families who had been affected by disparate sentencing laws, maltreatment while incarcerated, and issues the newly-released faced transitioning from a prison-to-freedom mindset. But then one person took the conversation entirely to the left with "stuff". I won't put that "stuff" here because it was waaayyyy out there. But it was enough that most of us fell silent (well, I was already silent) and crossed our fingers, toes, and eyes hoping the lady would finish up and sit down soon. A few of the members looked to me to say something; I'm a lawyer, have done plenty of pro bono work, have written articles for and worked with several civil rights and advocacy groups, so I should be saying something . . . right? Nope, I wasn't 'bout to get caught up in that! So, the moderator got us back on track and we finished up.

I thought I'd dodged a bullet, but then I received The

Text. Ms. Nellie asked how my day was going and hoped that I wasn't working too hard, then laid it on me: "Love, why didn't you speak up yesterday during the meeting? We were looking for your leadership."

Dandelions Always Make Noses ITch, i.e., DAMN IT!

Ms. Nellie looks good, but she's old enough to be my mom (her daughter and I are the same age). So, I couldn't blow her off, nor could I pretend like I didn't know what she was talking about. So, I told the closest thing to the truth I could think of: I wanted to be supportive and not take over the meeting.

I mentioned she was old enough to be my mom, right? So just like my mom, Ms. Nellie had no problem calling "BS" and letting me know it. I apologized and promised to do better in the future. And I did, but then another lesson came:

Leadership comes with truth, and some people can't handle the truth.

So, I thought I had this "sharing is caring" thing down pat. I'd synthesized my collective knowledge to create a bright line rule: If what I have to say is **informed**, **based on fact**, **said kindly**, and in a **safe spac**e, then it will be well-received and I will feel good about myself.

Uh-huh.

Not too long after I came up with that (now debunked) theory, I was talking with a friend who was also a business colleague about a project we'd been trying to get off the ground for literally a year. She had a business partner who I knew fairly well, but he left it to her to handle many administrative functions, and he handled the deals. After a year of us going around and around, with her promising to take our idea to him so we could move forward, I finally asked her if she wanted me to go to him directly. She was startled and offended. I couldn't really understand why because I used my new rule. During one of our work out sessions (safe space) I stated (kindly) that we had discussed this venture for a year (factual) and needed her partner's sign off to get it done (informed). I felt good. She, not so much.

My friend told me that she was a full partner in their business, didn't need his permission to do anything, if she hadn't believed in the project she'd have told me so, but if I insisted on talking directly with her partner, she would set it up (I think you know she did not). I tried to talk to her about the situation, but that's not where she was in life. But I understood where I was in life: I was in a place of truth.

The truth was that she wasn't a full partner in the business. At any time, her colleague could (and often did) reverse her decisions. She depended on her colleague to run payroll, as she had no access to the business' finances. And her colleague always introduced her as his subordinate – respectfully, but still as someone who worked for him – and she never corrected him.

And then it dawned on me why my friend was so mad. As long as I was content to go around and around with her about our project, she could continue to tell herself she was a partner. But once I pushed to speak with the person who ultimately could okay or kill the project once and for all, all hell broke loose.

1. EMBRACE THE SETUP SO YOU MAY BE SET LOOSE.

Our friendship cooled to a cordial acquaintanceship for over a year due to that dust up. I remember feeling frustrated and resentful that a relationship that I valued had been set back due to me breaking out of my shell and speaking up. But then I remembered that "A setback is a setup for a comeback," as Dr. Willie Jolley stated so eloquently. I was set up to shake off old ideas. I was set up to take back my voice and my time. I was set up to have a real, authentic relationship with my friend by removing the "project" dynamic so we could just be friends - people who go to lunch, giggle over headlines, and support one another through crisis. No more pretending. All that came from saying something, the *right* thing, that encompassed *everything.*

2. TRUST THE PROCESS - THERE IS A PLAN IN PLAY FOR YOUR GOOD.

I don't regret speaking up. I acknowledge and accept the consequences of standing up for myself and my time. And although I thought doing so had destroyed a valued friendship, I now realize that every action was a series of steps equivalent to a beautifully choreographed dance of celebration of my freedom.

Blessings in the Lessons

1. The truth does set you free, so make sure you have a parachute when you jump from Truth Air.
2. Relationships call EQ and IQ to engage in a two-step that many times looks like a war. Go with it and finish the dance, even if a few toes do get stepped on.
3. The world won't end no matter your individual decision. Take the stress off and do you.

CHAPTER 6

TIME VS. MIND CONSUMING: LIVE IN THE NOW, THE NEXT CAN WAIT

THERE ARE SO MANY SPECIAL MOMENTS of my daughter's life that I missed because I was working to build an empire. But if I had it to do all over again, I'd choose to build the empire slower and enjoy my daughter's tender years.

Many people don't tell this, but the truth is, I can't remember what I was doing or who I was meeting with or what conversation was so burningly important that I missed her kindergarten play, or her first grade Christmas party, or her first camping trip with the Girl Scouts. And because I feel the burn of missing those moments, I'm now VERY serious about how I spend my time. Most people are good with discerning tasks that are time consuming, but tasks that are mind consuming are equally dangerous.

A mind consuming task is one that distracts you from

your purpose. A mind consuming task is one that makes it difficult to determine next steps. A mind consuming task creates confusion for what you are and are not responsible.

Mind consuming tasks burn clocks, relationships, and businesses to the ground.

Why? Because there are many people who believe that if a task "only takes a few seconds" you should just do it and "keep it moving". Here's the thing: Just because something doesn't take you a lot of time doesn't mean it's not costing you money. And every time you refuse to delegate a task, you rob yourself of at least three types of opportunities.

The opportunity to expand your capacity to train better and cultivate a more patient spirit.

The opportunity to help someone learn a valuable skill and/or obtain more knowledge.

The opportunity to free your mind and time for other pursuits.

The last point is our area of focus. I know what it is to be so focused on getting things done that you don't want to take the time to hire someone else, much less the time to adequately train someone to do the job well. I know what it is to be so financially strapped that you commit to learning how to do things you NEVER had any interest doing because the only thing you had to pay someone with was a hug and smile…and you'd already used up all the grace the room had to offer. I know what it is to be so swamped in work you don't know where to start to even ASK someone to help you.

Take a breath. I've got you.

Literally, take 10 minutes and breathe.

Meditate. Clear your mind and give thanks. Thanks for being alive. Thanks for your family. Thanks for your business. Thanks for decisions that have yet to be made. Thanks for the presence of mind to pause.

Pray. Ask for clarity. Ask for wisdom. Ask for BOLD blessings. And expect to hear yes to your requests.

Now we can tackle the real issues.

You have people in your network who not only believe in you, they depend on you. They need your light, your brilliance, your determination, your positivity, your love, your grace, your kindness, your ideas, and your wisdom to make it through THEIR days. Tap them. Tell them what you need. This is no time for pride. You need help.

If you're working more than eight hours a day, you need help.

If you're skipping activities that you enjoy so you may work, you need help.

If you're missing your loved one's best moments, you need help.

Time waits for no (wo)man, and that includes you.

Take the time to train someone to help you so you CAN pay them to help. You'd be amazed at the number of people who are truly fascinated by what you do.

1. IF YOU'RE DOING IT RIGHT, THERE IS SOMEONE WHO CAN STEP IN FOR YOU.

I ran a media company for five years, and in the midst of it was diagnosed with stage 4 endometriosis. I resisted having surgery so long that the growth had wrapped around my intestines, encased my ovaries, and created a cement like sealant that bonded together my uterus, bowels, and vagina into one big blob. When I finally accepted that I needed a hysterectomy and would be down for almost two months, I didn't know how the magazines would go on. I was funding everything through my law firm, and while the firm would be fine while I recovered, that meant there wouldn't be any extra for the magazine. I prayed and asked the Lord for guidance and shared my concerns with a couple of our writers. And one rose – a Good man. David Good.

2. STEP BACK AND ALLOW YOUR HELP TO WORK THEIR MAGIC IN THEIR OWN WAY.

David took the helm of the magazines – all five of them – without pay for months. I was able to get back on my feet and we worked together to build the empire. He focused on the administrative side and I on the business development side. All the mind consuming work that had consumed me and kept me from getting out there and really working things were off my plate so I could turn my attention to developing partnerships, collaborative agreements, securing corporate sponsors, and growing from magazines to a full media agency. And the next year our lead title BOLD Favor was voted ATL's Hottest. Watch God work!

3. OUR HAPPINESS RESIDES IN NOW, NOT LATER.

And David grew from a writer to an editor to Editor-in-Chief to President of the firm. He implemented initiatives that included a full-figured calendar and more sponsors and red-carpet opportunities. And I was able to focus on the eternal moment of Now. My mind was (and is) with my daughter as we spend more time together making a mess in the kitchen cooking together (well, my version of it anyway), hanging out after school at the mall, and watching baking videos on YouTube on her oversized bean bag. Things that just a few years prior would have seemed crazy because I was trying to do everything myself, always thinking about Next and never able to enjoy what was happening right *now*.

It's not all gumdrops and lollipops, but life is "sho' nuff" more enjoyable sharing the load.

Blessings from the Lessons

1. We all need help sometimes, that is part of the lifecycle. You did not come into this world alone (thanks mom and dad!), and you will not live it that way either.

2. *Now* is all that matters. Planning for tomorrow should still be enjoyed in the moment of now. If whatever you set your mind to is robbing you of joy, let it go.

3. Breathe. Meditate. Pray. Always, every day.

CHAPTER 7

FIND A WAY. LIFE WAS CREATED WITH A THOUSAND HIDDEN PASSAGEWAYS

THERE WAS A TIME WHEN I WAS IN-house counsel for a private company and worked with a woman who, every morning, squeezed 30 minutes into her schedule to pass at least three Starbucks coffee shops to go to her coffee shop of choice because they made the best coffee in the world. This woman would order a large cup and divide it into three parts so that she could enjoy it all day.

One day the coffee shop changed their recipe and the coffee was not as good as it used to be. This woman got up 30 minutes earlier the next morning just to tell the store manager that she did not appreciate him changing her coffee. She informed the manager that she drives 30 minutes out of the way every day just to make sure she has their coffee. And that they needed to change the recipe back.

Guess what? They changed the recipe back to the original brew.

We complain about getting up early. We complain about our responsibilities. We complain about not having money. BUT if there's something that we REALLY want in life, we make it happen.

My former co-worker was the first to tell you she was not an early riser, yet she got up 30 minutes early every morning to drive out of her way to get a particular cup of coffee.

When I found out my daughter was on the way two days after turning in my letter of resignation so I could go it alone in my law firm, I didn't go back, I went forward and dug in. I didn't want to work for anyone else anymore. I wanted to put my time and talents to work for me and was willing to do whatever it took to make it happen.

When I was in college, people I knew for a fact were on financial aid, grants, work study, AND received public assistance somehow scrapped enough money together to go to Dayton Beach AND Freaknic every year.

So, don't accept excuses from folks about how they don't have or can't do. If there is something that a person really wants, he or she will find a way to make it happen.

Now the part none of us want to talk about is the

consequences of making something happen, the pain that naturally comes as the result of our decisions.

1. YOU'VE GOTTA GIVE SOMETHIN' TO GET SOMETHIN'.

For my co-worker, her pain was releasing her pillow 30 minutes earlier than normal just to get her coffee. She was willing to do it because she needed the caffeine to get through her day, to be bright and cheerful for the dozens of clients she needed to see, and to be energetic in facing whatever challenges would come her way (that sometimes included backed up toilets, moldy balconies, and missing pool passes during the hot Georgia summers).

2. DETERMINE THAT THE SACRIFICE IS WORTH IT.

For my college friends who made it to Spring Break destinations on a hope and somebody else's prayer, it was knowing when they got back they would be broke AND behind on their bills. They were willing to do it because they wanted to be a part of the crowd, to experience just a few days of just being a kid, without the worry of making the grades, cleaning up someone else's spills in the cafeteria, tutoring some spoiled prima donna in a subject she could care less about, or paying all those loans back with interest stacking up by the hour.

3. MASTER, CONTROL AND USE FEAR TO STAY FOCUSED AND MOTIVATED.

Building my law firm from the bottom up and not running back to my old job when I got scared meant embracing long days at the computer and cold calling large firms and title companies, running out of my comfort zone to meet new clients every day and learning new ways to bring value to the same processes so I could stand out, and knowing that there would be many family functions that I would miss (including my favorite little cousin's theatre debut – that still hurts today).

We all had a choice about how we would spend our time, talent, and resources, and we did it despite the pain that would come because we bet that the reward would be there.

But what happens when we bet it all on the horse and he doesn't deliver?

"You're not betting on the horse. You're betting on the jockey!" Lisa Nichols

That's right – you as the jockey still came through! You may not have gotten everything you wanted – winning the ultimate prize – but remember, you made it to the race! How many people never make it that far because they're not willing to even enter the race?!

You've gotta decide to get in there! You've gotta know you can win! You've gotta bet it all on finishing first! And if you don't this time, you go back and recalibrate and reenter and try again! And again! And again!

I took the CPA exam more than a couple of times before I passed. Guess what I became after the fifth time? A CPA!

I took the Bar twice before I passed. Guess what happened after I took it the second time? I became an attorney!

I've trained for a marathon twice, and only got up to completing a half-marathon. Guess what? Only 0.5% of the US population has ever completed a marathon and eventually, I'm going to do it!

You must be willing to embrace pain and USE IT to get what you want in life. Embrace the pain and watch the blessings rain!

Blessings from the Lessons

1. You were born with all the requisite knowledge, skills and connections to make "it" happen. You just need to put the pieces together in the right sequence for the magic to start.

2. For every action, there is an equal and opposite reaction. Some reactions take longer to manifest than others, but manifest, they must. You can and will handle it; you always do.

CHAPTER 8

PC DOESN'T BRING PEACE - BEING RIGHT VS. BEING CORRECT

NOT TOO LONG AGO, I HAD THE pleasure of participating in Career Day at a local elementary school. My escort for the day was a wonderful young man, a rising fifth grader. I was so impressed by his demeanor, beautiful manners, and charisma that I wanted to compliment his parents on what a wonderful job they were doing raising such a beautiful son. The guidance counselor shared with me some of the struggles they were having that included both parents suffering with kidney failure and the prospects of finding a match being remote because one of the parents had already donated a kidney to the other parent; multiple siblings for which my young man was responsible; and maintaining scholastics and sports excellence in spite of these hardships. Did I mention the school was taking up regular collections to ensure that my little guy's family had enough money for food?

My heart was broken, but I was determined to do something about it. I came out of that incredibly eye-opening experience with a determination to do something to help my little guy. At the time, I was running the media company, and I received a phone call from one of our writers. I really should have sent the call to voicemail.

The writer was upset because she did not like the magazine layout we used for her article. She went on to degrade the work of the other writers who'd contributed to the issue, the cover design, and the overall theme of the issue. Her exact words were, "I hate it, I really hate it."

I would normally just cut something like that off with a brusque comment, but not that day. I was emotionally compromised by the experience at the school and didn't want to use the filter I normally have in place to guard against saying things I may later regret. My EQ was in the negative digits.

1. HONESTLY ACKNOWLEDGE WHO YOU ARE AND WHERE YOU ARE IN LIFE AND YOUR BUSINESS' LIFE CYCLE.

I responded and it was bad. I didn't yell or curse, but it might have been better if I had. The coldness in my voice could have taken down the Night King in "Game of

Thrones". I was overly critical and very harsh. I felt justified because everything I said was true. In comparison to our other writers, she was one of the weakest we had, her work always needed significant edits – both grammatical and factual, and the pictures she submitted were of poor quality. However, when you're a small, start-up organization, you know that's something you're going to deal with. We were not *The Guardian* or *Essence*, and intellectually I knew that. It's one of the things that always made me so proud of our team - we loved helping one another. We had people in high school submit things to us, and coached and trained them up so now they are writing for other outlets, have created their own blogs, and one actually started a public relations agency.

And in that moment when I had an author going crazy, begging for coaching and correction and help… I blew it. I literally blew it up.

2. EXCUSE THE EXCUSES - THEY BLOCK YOUR ABILITY TO SEE CLEARLY AND TAKE DECISIVE ACTION.

I could use the excuse that I was upset, but life is full of upsets; people come to work after the death of a child or parent every day and give it their all, and you'd never know it.

I could use the excuse that I was defending the honor

of my organization and its people. Neither needed the defense. Organizations have no feelings, and our people were grown folks whose work clearly showed them to be exemplary professionals.

3. TRUTH IS NO EXCUSE FOR MEANNESS.

I could even say that everything I said to that writer was factually correct and I was simply walking in my truth, and anyone who can't take it can kick rocks.

But that's not my purpose, passion, or power, and I wasn't able to take bold or positive action.

My purpose is to strike the match and set people on fire with their reason for being. How in the world was I going to do that if I could not send one call to voicemail?

I knew I was upset. When the writer started talking, I knew I wasn't going to like what she had to say because she started with, "I don't know how to say this." It would have been so easy to just say, "Now is not a good time. Let's talk on Monday," and hang up. If I had it to do over again, that's exactly what I would have done. Because although hanging up without giving the person a chance to respond is politically incorrect, it would have been the right thing to do. It would have given both of us a chance to gather our thoughts, expend our negative energy, get a game plan as to how we wanted the conversation to end, and move on amicably afterward.

Thankfully, I learned from this experience. I now have no problem seeing a call and allowing it to go to voicemail, or answering a call and saying, "Let me call you back," when I know I'm not in the right frame of mind to deal with whatever is coming for me on the other end of the line.

By releasing the desire to be PC, your AQ emerges as a beacon of light that leads you back to the land of the reasonable and sensible.

Lessons from the Blessings

1. Being PC is overrated. If you have the choice between being right and being kind, choose kindness. You'll never regret it.
2. Every call does not need to be answered. There is a reason God made voicemail - use it.

CHAPTER 9

WHO CARES HOW YOU "MAKE IT", AS LONG AS YOU ARE "LAUGHING ALL THE WAY TO THE BANK"

WHEN MY DAUGHTER WAS LITTLE, she had a lot of hair, so I normally had someone else do it. Our normal hairdresser was down with a cold, so one of my girlfriends - T - heard the desperation in my voice when I asked her to please, please, PLEASE, do my baby's hair.

During the braiding process, we all got hungry, so we decided on barbeque and headed into the area of town we knew we'd find someone with a grill and some good sides. On our way, we passed a carwash that had been converted into a . . . wait for it . . . drive thru liquor store.

You know we had to go.

T whipped a quick U-turn I'm not sure was legal so we could go through the "store". The entire inside of the carwash was wall-to-wall alcohol. As the cars passed through, people hollered out your selections which were gathered by a very nice gentleman of Middle Eastern descent. Your items were totaled up, payment rendered and ta-da! Roll out, ready to enjoy your evening. But that's not all.

Once you exited the drive thru, there was a barbecue stand manned by a lovely African American family (dad was on the grill, mom was working the sides, children were working the flatware and plates) where you could pick up some ribs and chicken with maybe a side of garlic corn, potato salad, coleslaw, and excuse me - don't forget your dessert! Seeing as that was the original reason we'd ventured out, we loaded up. Once we had four bags of heart-attack-waiting-to-happen squared away, we proceeded toward the street to exit, but were once again sidelined by another nice gentleman, this one Caucasian, who asked if we needed an Amazon stick so we could enjoy some movies with our meal. I bought one just for the helluvit.

We picked up a nice bottle of wine, dinner, and a movie without leaving the carwash parking lot. Oh, I forgot to add that there was a DJ playing some nice family-reunion style music (I sang along to a couple of OJ's and Kool and the Gang songs while we waited for our food).

Now there were some people who passed by the carwash, pointing and laughing at the spectacle I just described. Truth be told, I chuckled more than one time as I considered where I was and what I was doing. Some people would say that converting a rundown carwash into three businesses was "ghetto", "country" or whatever other derogatory categorizations we come up with to describe things we feel are beneath us. But those people in that lot were able to take an abandoned building and convert it into something the community appreciated and supported. On Saturday night, people like to get a little wine and they are going to pick up food. They're probably going to watch a movie. And to keep people patient as they waited on their food, why not enjoy some music the entire family can enjoy.

I'm sure the team of people who came up with that arrangement took (and still take) more than their fair share of digs. People can be downright cruel. But when they go home at the end of the weekend, they have what those folks who were laughing wish they had – money. And instead of feeling embarrassed or low by those set downs, those savvy business owners are laughing, too – all the way to the bank.

Those business owners also did something that many communities can learn from – they found a way to work across cultural, racial, and most probably religious divides. They came together with their expertise to provide goods and services that people wanted and would pay for in a harmonious way. I am sure there were (and probably are) times when they look at one another in puzzlement as to why certain things are done certain ways, when they are inconvenienced by traditions that seem foreign, when feelings are hurt and offenses occur because of misunderstandings . . . yet they make it work. They found a way to make it work and to make a profit doing so. Those business owners allowed the sum total of their combined intelligence to "huddle up" for all their good.

Blessings from the Lessons

1. The only person's opinion that counts about your life and the way you live it is yours. Comedians aren't the only ones who laugh their way to the bank, but you'll only get there if you disregard the naysayers.

2. Try something new, team up with people in the vertical and horizontal pipelines of your business and industry - you may create your own Saturday Night hot spot.

CHAPTER 10

IF YOU WANT TO GET TO THE BOTTOM OF THINGS, DON'T GET MAD, GET NOSY

I HAVE A GIRLFRIEND WHOSE COUSIN would literally go to war for her. She has been there through the thick and thin. When both of them were unemployed at the same time, this girl's cousin made sure that her little cousin was taken care of. But then when everything seemed to settle down and they were both working good jobs, my friend's cousin started acting crazy. Crazy to the point where she told her that she needed one amount and then that amount literally was multiplied times 10 and she wouldn't return phone calls, would not respond to text messages, wouldn't respond to social media posts to talk about this issue. When my friend told me what happened, I told her, "Listen. This is bad. Something is wrong and you need to find out what it is." Don't get mad when people act crazy, get nosy!

Sometimes, it's the people closest to us who wound us deepest. Whether it's an overly harsh word or seeming lack of support when we do things, our friends and family members can cut us deep with the flick of the wrist. Our emotional guard is down because we feel comfortable, so a callous word has brutal consequences from a loved one, when the same would not even warrant a side eye from a stranger. However, I've had to learn that people's behavior is about THEM not about me, no matter who "people" are.

What does that mean?

We are the sheroes of our lives. Everything is viewed through our own lenses. It's rare that a person is able to remove her own spectacles, put on someone else's, and see clearly. What normally happens is that we have a distorted view of what we THINK is going on, but without guidance (i.e., corrected medicine in the lens), what we see is not the reality of what is.

I have a challenge for you that will both bless you and hurt you, but it will ultimately enable you to help the person you love, and your capacity for empathy and compassion will grow. Truly, you'll be an AQ All-star. Are you ready?

When people act out of character, find out why.

When someone you love and who you know loves you starts acting in a peculiar way, don't get mad - get NOSY! Get all into their business. I'm talking about full body cavity search. I'm talking about your-mother-rifling-through-your-stuff kind of nosy. I'm talking about your neighbor-who-was-always-outside-trying-to-see-what's-going-on-at-your-house nosy. I'm talking about total-complete-violation-of-your-privacy nosy!

I know this sounds out of the box, crazy, and downright creepy "single white female"; but please believe me when I say that when someone you love shows out on you, they are crying out for help. If someone normally behaves one way and turns cray-cray in 60 seconds flat, something is wrong, and you need to find out what it is.

1. DETERMINE HOW YOU CAN HELP.

My friend took the challenge and called her cousin from an unfamiliar number. (Yep, you might have to do it! If you're in town, the pop up is good, too!) When my friend finally got her cousin on the phone and asked her directly what's wrong and HOW CAN I HELP, her cousin broke down and told her what was going on.

Did you see that part in all caps? She asked how she could help. My friend didn't accuse her bestie of lying, didn't throw recriminations at her, didn't condemn her behavior . . . she asked how they could work TOGETHER to dig out of this hole she found herself in.

Now, it doesn't always turn out as well as it did for

my friend. I know because I have the scars to prove that sometimes people lash out hard when they're cornered. I have a friend who was married to a nice guy. I knew they were having trouble long before the divorce because her appearance had started to decline. I'd known my friend several years and she NEVER left the house looking less than her best – even to the grocery store. But one day she came over to my house with her ponytail askew, unwashed face, and wrinkled clothing. I was stunned. I asked her if her husband was out of town, and she told me he would be home in about an hour. I swallowed, blinked, and gave her a look (like only we women can give one another!) and asked her if she was going to get herself together before he got home. She said to me, "Girl, he takes what he gets."

Oh man.

So, right here I gotta tell ya that sometimes I'm looking pretty rough around the edges at home. I'm HOME. But she wasn't home, she was out running errands. I'm her buddy, but she'd made stops – plural – before coming to my house and had another to make before she went home. When I add this to the fact that this is the same person who wouldn't come down the stairs to greet her guests at HER party because she couldn't get this ONE strand of hair in the BACK of her head to lay down just right . . . I knew we were in emergency mode.

So, I asked her what was going on. I reminded her men were visual and before her hubby got home, she needed to get it together a bit (it was a reminder because this is something we'd discussed several times through the years when we'd see people out and about looking any-kinda-way and then post on social media "I don't know why I can't find a nice guy"). I then asked how I could help. It didn't go well. She got mad. REALLY MAD. She sucked her teeth, rolled her eyes, and left without another word.

2. BE READY TO ACCEPT THE CONSEQUENCES OF WHAT COMES NEXT.

She didn't speak to me for two years.

It really hurt. We talked at least three times a week. Her number was one of the few I knew by heart in the age of digital convenience. We went out and hung out as couples. My circle of real friends is very small, so to lose a link in the chain was devastating. I FELT THAT. After going through anger and pain and anger, I finally settled on acceptance and went on with my life.

3. ACCEPT THE OLIVE BRANCH WITH GRACE, WHENEVER IT COMES.

Then one day out of the blue she called me. I was shocked, but I answered the phone because I missed my friend. It was very awkward; a lot of the high-pitched,

"Hey how're you doing?" "Fine, how are you?" that hide the real questions "Girl, where've you been?" "Why'd you go missing?!" Neither one of us are fake people, so the pleasantries didn't last long. Finally, we were silent, and I waited. She asked if she could come over, and when she arrived 10 minutes later, the dam broke: Her husband had become a real boob.

Cheated. Was paying his mistress' bills while the home he shared with his wife – my friend – foreclosed. Had a baby. Had two families. Wanted her to become a pseudo-Sister Wife.

Whatever hurt feelings I had before we sat down washed away in the torrent of feelings my friend had to have experienced during all this time. She'd been dealing with all this alone and it had started – you guessed it – when she lashed out. It was too much to share because she was internalizing these issues. She'd been trying to fix things herself. If I've not learned anything else these 20 plus years of marriage, I've learned that marriage requires your real friends to hold you up . . . and slap your crazy butt upside the head every once in a while to straighten you out. I can't say with certainty that the four of us having a conversation in faithful solidarity would have stopped them from breaking up, but they would have known that they weren't alone in the struggle to save 25 years of love. And we could have fought TOGETHER.

So now I take very seriously asking people what's

up, investigating until I get an answer that makes sense, working to see how I may assist, staying out and praying for the situation when I see there isn't anything for me to do and allowing the Lord to do what He does best – work it out for all our good.

Blessings from the Lessons

1. Real friendship requires real conversations to get to the heart and soul of a matter. If a person acts out of character, they are NOT alright and things are not all right.

2. Your life experience is about you. You draw people into that experience to learn and grow. Doing "nothing" does not help you with your mission. Stop standing on the sidelines being PC, roll up your sleeves and get to work on your mission.

CHAPTER 11

DOWN WITH THE ISMS (RACISM, SEXISM, AGEISM...)

"The world will not be destroyed by those who do evil, but by those who watch them without doing anything." Albert Einstein

MY DAUGHTER CAME HOME ONE DAY and told me that one of her friends said they couldn't be friends because her dad didn't want her to be friends with black people. She stated it so matter-of-factly that I needed a moment to process what she'd said. Since she said it without much emotion – as if she were reporting the weather – I proceeded to conduct my undercover examination in the same manner. I asked her what she thought about that, how did it make her feel, how did she and her friend come to that subject of conversation, if her friend believed her father was right, would they remain friends, was she afraid of her friend's father ...?

My daughter is a smart little cookie, and one of the most beautiful human beings I've ever encountered. She could see that as calm as I was, that I was close to the edge, and worked to assure me that she understood that racism was wrong, that it made her sad that people were racist but she knew that most people were good, her friend knew her father was wrong in his thinking, that they would remain friends, and that she knew I would come for that man if he ever made a move on my baby. I let it go and sent her on her way to enjoy video games and YouTube videos.

But I didn't really let it go.

As an African-American woman in her 40's, I've experienced a degree of hurt from people who've judged me to be less than, incompetent, undeserving, and lacking – so much that it makes my throat constrict and tears come to my eyes. Although many years have passed since a high school teacher's spittle landed on my face in the middle of his lecture and he laughed (inciting the rest of the class to laugh); since a manager who'd never met me told a room of other managers that a mentor wouldn't have helped me because I was just not the right fit for the firm (even though all my peers had a mentor); since a selection committee reviewed my credentials and told me I was amazing, but not as good as a person 10 years my junior . . . because she was 10 years younger; it still burns. But not because those actions and words and thoughts resonate with me. Rather, it's because I know my daughter will face these challenges one day, and I fear that my preparations to fortify her will not be enough.

I started thinking and considering what led an Asian man in these United States to feel so superior that he would judge a child as less than? The answer was uncomfortably familiar. At the core of racism is pain. There's ignorance, too, because the pain is directed to the wrong source, but at the core is pain. That man was in pain. Someone had mistreated him or someone he loved. Someone convinced him that the person who caused the pain was the model for an entire group of people, that the entire group was responsible for the pain, and given the chance would hurt him again. And he chose to protect himself from the pain by painting a broad X over an entire race of people as a cautionary sign so he'd never experience that kind of pain again.

1. ALLOW YOUR PAST TO PROVIDE CONTEXT AND UNDERSTANDING.

I understood because I've felt close to doing the same several times in my own life. I never did because I was raised in a home full of love and forgiveness. I took those lessons into my adulthood, and allowed my AQ to bring to the forefront of my mind instances when I said things and did things that did not live up to the expectations or training my family had for me or instilled in me; and yet, I was extended grace anyway.

Grace, by a manager when I messed up a project and she had to fix it, but took time to show me what I did wrong and how to avoid it, and didn't nail me on my performance review . . . and took up for me during the same meeting when the manager told the room that a mentor wouldn't have helped me. She was Caucasian.

Grace, by a young writer I'd failed as a mentor during her early months in the profession not making the time to meet on a regular and consistent basis to really help her launch as powerfully as she should have . . . yet she always thanked me and never called me out for what I could have and should have done. She was in her early twenties.

Grace, by a friend when I made a careless comment impugning his religion. He corrected me firmly and moved on in the conversation, never mistreating me or allowing that one thing to damage or derail our relationship. My friend is Asian.

So, when I thought about my own experiences and my own shortcomings, I understood where my daughter's friend's dad was coming from. I didn't like it, hated actually, but I understood. And in understanding, I knew I had a call to action.

2. BE THE CHANGE YOU WANT TO SEE IN THE WORLD AND BRING IT WITH JOY.

In our house, we had a saying. "I'm gonna show you better than I can tell you." It means I'm going to prove what I can do rather than talk about it.

So that's what I decided to do. Instead of raising my daughter with fear at the core of every experience I wanted her to have, I'd raise her with love and grace radiating through her core. When she encounters those who will treat her in a way that shows THEIR pain, that she would be excellent, yet merciful. Excellent in that she will give her best (with the understanding that one's best changes depending on the situation at hand, resources and assistance available, and life challenges at play); merciful in that she wouldn't seek revenge for injustices dealt to her, but rather seek justice.

Revenge saps the spirit, eroding creativity and innovation. It robs us of our abilities to bring forth the best of ourselves and others.

Justice empowers the spirit, emboldens us toward perfection, energizing us to be ultimate creators and innovators. It lights the fires within and inspires others to want more for themselves and others, and to work hard for it.

I want justice.

With justice comes peace and love and joy. Peace to

forgive and move on. Love to embrace and serve those who haven't quite made it "here". Joy to do it all just for the love of it (but happy to get paid to do it!).

Embrace the pain and watch the blessings reign.

Blessings from the Lessons

1. Treat others as you want to be treated - with compassion and true care.

2. You control you and only you. Keep both hands on your life steering wheel, focus on the road, and no texting while living.

3. We protect ourselves and our children by teaching them (and ourselves) that no one is exempt from pain, but everyone is equipped with the tools to transform pain into joy.

CHAPTER 12

NO ONE KNOWS WHAT YOU'RE GOING THROUGH UNTIL YOU TELL THEM ... SO TELL IT ALL

AT THE HEIGHT OF MY BATTLE WITH endometriosis, I realized I was going to have to make a decision on how I was going to proceed with comments about my weight, and I didn't really like my options.

I was shopping at a boutique and wanted to try on a dress. It was beautiful and (I thought) made of material that had some "give". I'd shopped at this boutique on many occasions and the owner and I were on very good terms. With all the treatments and stress and pain of endometriosis, I had gained a significant amount of weight. I didn't realize how much until that day because I was pretty much wearing the same clothes – those that didn't require me to wear a brassiere and had a lot of give.

I had gotten to a place where I couldn't wear anything that constricted me or contoured to my body.

So, it wasn't until I picked up a particular outfit and was just looking at it to see if it had any "give" that I came to My Moment of Truth. The boutique owner made the comment, "Now that's tight on me, so come on now." And it really hurt my feelings. How could she say such a thing? Didn't she know what I was going through? The nights that I couldn't sleep I was in so much discomfort. The periods that were so raw I traded my sanitary napkins for Depends diapers. The wigs I wore to hide my broken and damaged hair. How could she? Didn't she understand?!

When you gain weight, you don't necessarily realize it until your clothes get tight, and even then, there's a part of you that is in utter denial about it because it really could be that your dryer is shrinking your clothes.

But it's even worse when you are suffering from an illness and your body is going crazy. It makes you insane when people remark upon your weight gain (and I suspect the same is true for a person going through weight loss for the same reason). You take the knocks and don't say much about why you're gaining (or losing). Our ego tells us that it's easier to allow people to believe you're overeating than to let them in on your health challenges. Acknowledging something is wrong and the doctors don't know what it is or how to fix it is scary. You don't want to talk about it with random people because you're doing your best to be "normal" (whatever that means!) and get through it. Your AQ can't start to work on your healing because your emotions must work through their processes. But once that is complete, help and health can and will manifest.

1. SPEAK UP AND LET IT OUT.

No, the boutique proprietress didn't understand. No, she didn't know what I was going through. I'd never TOLD HER. My ego wouldn't let me.

I was pretending things were fine, ignoring the pain, rescheduling doctors' appointments, blowing off holistic solutions, and being a downright crazy person in my approach to managing my illness.

I was at the proverbial fork in the road. Did I want to say something or stay buttoned up? I needed time to think. I put the item back and wound up not purchasing anything. On the way home, I thought about how I was going to handle my new normal. I told my ego to sit down and yield to the God in me - my AQ.

2. TAKE CONTROL OF YOUR HEALTH AND WELL-BEING WITH ENTHUSIASM AND ZEAL.

I decided that I was going to focus on getting better with the same intensity I used to get through every other thing in life I ever wanted and got done. I pushed my doctors to get creative and travel the road less-traveled in getting to a diagnosis. That led to the truth of my condition and surgery and many days feeling like I wanted to die, but I got to the bottom and was able to push my way back up to the surface.

I decided that I was going to share my condition and the hardships that came with it with those who were bold enough to make comments. Those comments sometimes were indirect ("You don't look like yourself") and direct ("That's a little tight on you"). That led to more people talking about endometriosis, coming to realize that they aren't crazy and there IS something to be done to minimize the pain.

3. SET GOALS TO ACHIEVE AND THINGS TO ENJOY ONCE YOU COME THROUGH THE HARDSHIP.

I decided that I was going to buy that dress in the boutique as a beacon of hope to WHEN I would be better. I needed something tangible to look forward to and decided I'd wear it one day – even if it was only for an hour - when I got better. And I did. And it really was for only an hour because I couldn't stand the undergarments I had to wear to "smooth things out". Ha!

Although the experience was incredibly painful, and I continued to have challenges due to my illness even after surgery, I don't regret or begrudge a single moment.

One thing pain can do is make you more empathetic and compassionate, pulling up your AQ to genius level. Endometriosis has really given me a level of empathy and compassion for people who suffer on every level – physical, mental, emotional, and spiritual.

It's also made me more positive about the world. I know we have A LOT of problems in our world, but there is also beauty. I work hard to find the beauty in people and to remark upon it. And if I don't have something positive to say, many times I don't say anything at all. I understand the power of words. I understand that life and death are in the power of my tongue, that I have the ultimate power to breathe blessings over a person or curses that destroy her soul.

And I realized that I could build an empire with only my heart and tongue. Small things amount to big things over time. The ant hill is made of individual grains of sand. That hill is strong and deep, and hard to totally destroy (ask any gardener or pest control professional!). A sincere compliment is a grain of sand. Genuine support of an idea is a grain of sand. Introduction of two people with like minds is a grain of sand. These are the building tools to creating a fortress of success.

4. EMBRACE AND REVEL IN THE NOW.

I embrace where I am in life and the people around me. I embrace what I've been able to do and acknowledge the things that fell through the cracks. I embrace the person I am and one day will be. But it came after I made a decision as to how I was going to deal with my pain.

Embrace the pain and watch the blessings reign.

Blessings in the Lessons

1. Joy truly comes in the morning, but you have to make the journey "through" the night (challenge), open your eyes to the breaking of day (your new course of action) and get up and live the day.

2. People's comments hurt us when there is subconscious doubt in our minds holding that same position. Face it, determine the root cause of it, embrace it and let it go.

3. Your ego is an unsupervised child running around in your mind. Grab her hand, tell her you love her, sit her down and that Mommy's got it from here.

CHAPTER 13

SHAKE UP THE TEAM IF YOU WANT TO GROW, I.E., DOWN WITH THE CLIQUE

WHEN I WAS IN COLLEGE, I APPLIED to and was denied membership in a sorority. The denial hurt, but the worst pain came when a couple of my friends were admitted and started acting "funny". I made a decision that I would never treat others that way.

And then I did.

I have been blessed to do some really cool things in my life and through my businesses. One of the best was the US Small Business Administration ChallengeHer program. Companies applied to host competitions all over the country to find innovative ideas to help women balance the work-family-life challenge. (I know now that there is no such thing as life balance, only aggregate intelligence shifting priorities as life demands. But I was still learning!) I was so happy because my company was still small and growing, so to be approved was beyond exhilarating. I got the email while on the phone with my friend Elaine and almost busted her eardrum with my piercing scream of delight. Sorry Elaine!

In getting the various committees together to host a powerful challenge (planning, application, sponsorship, prizes, communication, and hospitality); I reached out to my tried and true friends and colleagues. It never occurred to me to ask anyone else to take part. And I never would have if I hadn't received a text message from a colleague saying she wanted to be down.

What?

I had formed a clique. I didn't realize it because my clique was the group of people I know would support just about anything that I do. I didn't realize it because we always do really big and really, really cool things together. But I should have realized it because it was just the same people in the group. That is kind of the definition of a clique.

It hit me like a ton of bricks what I had done. And I had to face it and own it because the person who said it was right. And I had to face how much I was limiting the work I was doing by keeping my circle so close and closed.

There's a right way to address anything - and sometimes it's privately.

I really appreciated and admired the way my colleague approached me. She sent me a private message, very respectfully stating that she would love to be included in my planning and my community groups, but she wasn't sure what was required. Was there a membership fee or was it free? I had to catch my breath. Of course there was no membership fee to be in my circle and yes, of course, it was free. And I told her that. And I was honest in my reply when I told her that literally it's people I know and trust and will almost certainly say "Yes" to whatever wild and crazy scheme I come up with next! And, of course, she was relieved to know that and I told her that I was happy to include her on my next wild and crazy and zany idea - including this one.

The experience really set me for a loop and I remembered how I felt in college all those years ago with the sorority. I had a new empathy and appreciation for my friends who got caught up in the newness of their group. And I understood the power of The Clique – in trying to be "down" with the clique, it could bring your whole world crashing down around you.

2. THE CIRCLE CHANGES AS YOU CHANGE - IT IS A LIVING, BREATHING THING THAT PARALLELS YOUR LIFE.

It's imperative to reach outside of your circle and ask people to join in on initiatives and projects if you're serious about growing and expanding your territory "indeed". Ask people to get involved and give them the opportunity to say "No" or to not come through. If they say "Yes" and do what they said they'd do, you have new resources to tap and learn from. If they say "No" or don't live up to their commitments, it gives you an opportunity to ask someone else or learn a new skill yourself. Either way, you're going to be alright!

The clique can be deadly. It leads to groupthink (think The Challenger). It leads to stealing ideas because there's no new energy and innovation in the group (think boy bands in the 90's). It leads to a lack of creativity and ingenuity. It leads to a lack of empathy and compassion for those outside of the group. All of these things lead to reduced life success, i.e., AQ. The higher the aggregate intelligence, the better your life purpose comes into relief. The opposite is also true: the lower your AQ, the less satisfaction and joy you feel in life because your purpose is suppressed.

3. ALWAYS BOLO FOR POSSIBLE PITFALLS.

At the time of that incident, I had not had my "group" long enough for those things to really become an issue. I'm always looking for the next thing to get my hands into, I'm always meeting new people and trying new ideas. But my colleague's message really brought me to the place where I realized that it could become an issue and that is just not something that I want.

So now I reach out to people and ask them if they'd be interested in partnering up. I make open calls for inclusion in my projects and initiatives. And I'm sincere in my efforts to weave ideas that aren't my own into the fabric of my work so that everyone sees their contributions – whether a single thread or an entire pattern of the tapestry. It's hard, I won't lie to you. I get tired and frustrated, and sometimes I just want to push people to the side and get it done myself. But then I can't expand.

When I pray in the mornings, I ask God to "bless me indeed". The indeed blessing requires financial and human resources. If I'm constantly doing things myself, or it's the same people doing everything, then there isn't any ROOM for anything else. As part of the same prayer, I ask for wisdom and protection. God won't give me the "indeed" until I get the infrastructure in place to receive it. When I see things stagnating, things won't move or "break", I look at the system and support I have in place and see what needs to be tweaked. There's always something that needs to be improved, a person who needs encouragement, an email service that needs to be replaced, a payment system that needs to be upgraded, or I need rest and rejuvenation . . . and sometimes all of the above.

The Clique experience was enlightening. I don't regret it and realized that it could and possibly would happen again (and it did). It happened when I was over extended and didn't want to take on something (or someone) else who was untested into my tenuously balanced life. But that, in itself, was a lesson because it meant I needed to take more time to grow responsibly – over time, and with my health and family at the center.

I don't know it all, and I'm learning as I go. I choose to embrace the pain so I can learn for my ultimate gain!

Blessings from the Lessons

1. Include at least one new person in your group every time you do something new. That person's ideas, network connections, and strategies will surprise and delight you.

2. Your hurt today can lead to someone else's injury tomorrow. Don't be too hard on yourself or your tormentor. We're all learning together as we play the Game of Life for the ultimate prize of optimal AQ.

CHAPTER 14

TAKE A MOMENT AND CONSIDER: THE BLOCKS ARE ALSO PROTECTIVE BARRIERS

SOMETIMES WE THINK PEOPLE IN FRONT of us are holding us back when, really, they are providing us with protection.

I was driving one morning on my way home from working out with a friend and there was a police car in front of me. So, of course, I was taking extra care to allow for the allotted number of cars in front of me and driving according to the speed limit. There was a person behind me who was driving rather aggressively, and I know that that person couldn't tell that the car in front of me was a police car. Although the police car was marked as such, it did not have any lights on top and the body was not the standard sedan.

So, the person behind me decided that she wanted to get in front and she came around me very quickly and whipped in front of me. She immediately realized that she was behind the cop, and that the officer had probably seen what she had done (which was just this side of legal). She started driving very cautiously, giving the allotted space between cars and according to the speed limit.

See, what she thought was me holding her up in the morning and getting in the way of her starting her day was actually protection from probably getting a ticket, or worse yet, running straight into that cop's car when he came to a stop at some yellow light that she thought he should have pushed through.

1. DETERMINE IF IT IS IT A BLOCK OR A PROTECTIVE SHIELD . . . OR BOTH?

Many times, we think God is doing the same thing - blocking our paths, standing in our way - when we think we know best. I've asked for things, but can't see what He sees, can't know why things are happening as they are occurring. It is at those times that we must trust in the Lord with all our hearts and all our souls, knowing that He is working for our good and that it is intentional.

That is a hard lesson to implement in life, particularly in one's professional life. We are taught to be aggressive and go after every endeavor full steam ahead, and not allow anything to stand in our way – not even our good sense. We have claimed others' ideas as our own in the name of expediency, we've blown off meetings with one contact to meet with someone of perceived greater importance, and we've kept our word pushing through to the end of some project even after variables have changed and the ground is falling out from under us. In each instance, we look at what is happening (or not happening) as a road block instead of pausing to evaluate the cause. Could that idea have been a poison pill to our organization? Could that meeting with the first contact have been the network connection breakthrough we'd been looking for? Was that change in circumstance the final stop sign needed to prevent catastrophe? How do we know when an event takes place to help us and not to harm us? How do we know our ego has not hijacked the car (our AQ) and taken us hostage?

2. TRUST, BUT VERIFY.

We must test it.

I'd tell you to trust your gut, but sometimes the rumblings in your belly really are just gas. When you're unsure, you've got to put it out there and see what's going on. You've got to test the waters.

When that woman swerved around me to speed past me, she was testing the situation. The only way for her to know for a fact that there was a reason that I was not going faster was for her to see for herself. Some experiences only yield knowledge when one goes through them personally.

3. ALLOW TIME TO DO ITS JOB AND TELL THE ULTIMATE TALE.

The test comes in trusting that no matter what happens, you're going to be **all** right. That's not a typo – I really do mean that you will be **all well**, that all things will work toward your total good, and that everything you're striving to achieve that is in your best interest will come to pass at the right time. That is a boldly audaciously simplistic way of looking at things, but it's true. And you know that deep in your heart, otherwise you would not have ever risked trying. Just like that woman who went around me.

And just as that driver went around me, took the lay of the land and adjusted her plan with the new information before her, i.e., the police officer in front of her; so, too, will you adjust your plans and actions when presented with life's unexpected gifts. And you will be just fine. ALL right.

Blessings from the Lessons

1. Trust, but verify, when you're not sure. If it can't stand up to scrutiny, then "it" isn't for you. Keep going until you find the right "it".

2. Life is more than "right" and "wrong"; it includes "right now", "wrong way", "right here", and "no right", and "two wrongs" to name a few ways we get ourselves in and out of mischief. Take time to figure out which right or wrong statement applies - if any.

CHAPTER 15

EXPERIENCE, WISDOM, AND NEW VENTURES COME FROM THE VALLEY EXPERIENCE, I.E., I FEEL YOUR PAIN

I RECEIVED AN EMAIL FROM AN ORGANIZATION, actually a magazine, recognizing me for an honor. When I went online to ensure that it was credible, I found mixed reviews. Most of the negative (all that I read, but after a while, I stopped reading because they were all the same) were from people who appeared to be upset that they did not feel special "enough". Their particular gripe was that they had to pay a fee to have their profile included in the magazine and to receive the other honoraria that went with it. None of the reviews I read said anything about the magazine not being credible, not delivering on what it promised, and not actually going to print. As a matter of fact, the organization had been in business quite some time, and the positive reviews all spoke to the integrity

LYNITA MITCHELL- BLACKWELL

of the team and the business leads that came due to the profiles.

I felt that organization's pain. Acutely.

At the time, I was running my own media company, publishing multiple magazines, I felt strong compassion for that organization. A lot of times people forget that it costs money to produce these wonderful honors and awards programs. Whether they are print or live events, they all cost money . . . but the entire experience got me to thinking about the fact that sometimes there may be a voice of truth in the jungle of noise . . . and maybe when the organization started off it wasn't legitimate.

1. REMEMBER WHERE YOU CAME FROM, COMPASSION AND EMPATHY TAKE ROOT AT THE BEGINNING OF YOUR STORY.

So, I went back.

I went back to that organization's first issue and read through it. I went through most editions through the years, and just like most organizations that start with "$2.00 and a dream", the first issue was rough, but as the organization grew, the quality of the magazines also improved. It was interesting because I thought about my own organization's ups and downs in publishing our magazines, and how every title we'd put out went through the same process. I applied that knowledge to the situation at hand and judged the organization's presentation over the past year. And I found what I expected - the magazine that I reviewed over the past year was full of very nice articles as well as profiles of exceptional professionals. Truly a beautiful read.

2. THERE IS VALUE IN THE VALLEY.

I took time to explore that organization's Valley Experience, and in so doing really embraced my own.

There's value in the unknown, also known as the Valley. The Valley is hard because it's uncomfortable and unfamiliar. Don't try to skip past it – go through it. Go through the hard parts. Don't always try to find a short cut. There's experience in the valley, knowledge and wisdom to be gained while in the valley. New relationships to forge and some to leave behind as you trek through the valley. And once all has been gained from the valley, and you leave it behind, you'll never have to return.

Take time to learn all you can while in the valley. When you try something new, you won't know what you're doing - it's new! - and you won't have all the answers. You don't need all the answers. And people are going to evaluate you using criteria that may or may not make sense to you, that you may or may not understand. It's okay. Learn to see both sides of an issue, and not favor one over the other. Then you'll be able to provide value to your target client, not "everybody" because you can't please "every body". Last, take time to take your next step. You don't have to move immediately. You can take time to deliberate. If something has to be moved on "right now", then it probably isn't for you "right now".

In taking the time to really review and understand that organization's journey, I felt gratitude for my fellow journeymen and women, the people who hung in there with us through our ups and downs, gratitude for our advertisers and subscribers who invested in us through our struggles and challenges, and gratitude for our writers who were proud to be affiliated no matter what was – or was not – going on.

3. DECIDE HOW YOU WANT TO FEEL, THEN DISOWN ANYTHING THAT IS CONTRARY TO THAT FEELING.

And I chose to feel honored by that organization that reached out to me. I chose to feel special. I did not choose to not feel "special enough". Nor did I choose to feel that what they were offering was not good enough. I also chose to feel compassion and to commit to allowing that feeling to flow into other areas of my life.

In taking control of my feelings, i.e., making a choice as to what I would allow to flow through my consciousness, I determined my destiny. My AQ increased, and I was able to see the hard work and quality in that publication.

A lot of times we are so fixated on the fact that an offer is non-exclusive we forget that the thing offered is of significant value – that "something" was still a gift from someone's heart. It's not a betrayal when someone makes simultaneous offers. It's an acknowledgement that while some people will see the value in what we have, others will not, and we're not sure where a certain person will fall on the spectrum.

Blessings in the Lesson

1. Valley Experiences are critical tools to climb over plateaus and break through ceilings. Take a breath, focus on the task at hand and work.

2. You determine your destiny through your thoughts and feelings. "As a man thinketh, so shall he be," is not just a cute tee-shirt saying. Decide what you want, then take action.

CHAPTER 16

TAKE THE ZEAL AND THE WILL; ALLOW FRUSTRATION TO BURN OFF EVERYTHING ELSE

WHEN MY DAUGHTER WAS SMALL, she volunteered to participate in a spelling bee. That means that I volunteered to be in the spelling bee, too.

1. PUT IN THE WORK.

We studied every day for three weeks, over 1300 words. I was very proud of her and the effort that she put forth to ensure that she was as prepared as possible. The problem was that the people who coordinated the spelling bee did not make every effort to ensure that the program would be executed smoothly and that the students could do as well as they possibly could.

The person that the organization selected to call the words had not prepared for the task. Her diction was terrible. Now this is something big for me to say because in all the years that I had been speaking up to that point, the thing that I had been criticized for most in my delivery was my diction. Sometimes I was so excited about what I had to say that I'd just talk and didn't necessarily take the time to ensure that what I was saying was actually being understood. But after that experience, I do now! (There's something about someone messing with your kids that sets you straight.) And so, when I know that someone's performance is based upon me and something that I'm saying, I take the time to ensure that what I'm saying is understood.

But back to the lesson.

2. FOLLOW THROUGH, EVEN WHEN IT SEEMS ONLY DISASTER WILL RESULT.

That spelling bee caller mispronounced words so badly that twice the organizer had to come over to look at the card to see what the poor lady was trying to say. I got madder and madder as the rounds went on. We'd made it to round seven, and a child had been eliminated on every subsequent round trying to spell words this woman was mispronouncing. I was really about to lose my mind! And then it was time for my baby to fall victim to the injustice. The caller mispronounced the word and my daughter, who is a determined and tough little cookie, gamely tried to spell this word she didn't recognize and of course misspelled it.

I was so pissed. We'd worked so hard for so long on all those words, only to be eliminated by this person who couldn't pronounce the words! But I couldn't lose it in front of my daughter. I took her out of the room and I told her how proud I was of her and that she did really well. And she did! I had to focus on the hard work and dedication she put forth – voluntarily – at age 8 during her summer vacation to make her dream of winning a spelling bee come true. And I told her that sometimes we do everything in our power to make things come true, but there are external forces that can get in our way. Those things can't impact who we are inside, but sometimes impact the results of our efforts. We must strive for perfection anyway.

When I focused on the experience from that perspective, I realized that I was talking to myself as well as my daughter. It was a learning experience for both of us and one that my daughter did not forget.

3. MAKE BETTER DECISIONS BASED ON WHAT YOU LEARNED AND KNOW NOW.

The next year when the organizers came to my daughter and asked her to participate in the bee, she emphatically refused. I supported that decision 100%. It was only after she refused and I backed her refusal that I asked her why she said no. My daughter informed me that the amount of work that she would need to put in during her summer vacation to ensure she would do well was not worth what she knew was going to be presented to her – that same caller was returning. And that was absolutely right. My daughter learned a very valuable lesson at an early age: Before we expend a whole lot of effort to do something that is near and dear to our hearts, we have to ensure the people who are responsible for judging us and our performances are worthy of that post. If not, we find another way to share our gifts and accomplish our goals.

And my daughter did . . . in design. Instead of studying for the spelling bee that summer, she taught herself to draw clothing designs and worked with my dress designer to bring them to life. I was so proud of her!

If you were to ask my daughter today whether she regretted the Bee experience, she will tell you that she doesn't even remember it. My daughter released the frustration of the loss, but not the zeal, discipline and energy that experience created within her. She simply redirected it into another gift, one over which she has much more control to share with others.

Our aggregate intelligence allows us to be whole in all things, successful in all things, even when it seems we have come up short. That is because our life purpose is not to win, but to create. The first verse of the Bible is "In the beginning, God created . . ." and later in Genesis, He created man and woman in His image. That means we were gifted with the ability to create new things from the old - or in this instance with my daughter, to create clothing using the zeal developed from conditioning for the spelling bee.

Blessings from the Lessons

1. You can do anything when your will and zeal partner up. Your spirit is allowed to flow, and frustrations fall away, leaving only the experience and wisdom gained from the Valley Experience. This experience and wisdom are tools to be utilized to accomplish your goals.

2. Failure is not the end. It is only the beginning of the next journey. If you haven't made it to your ultimate destination, then the energy must be used for something else. Stay focused so that your gifts are used wisely and for good while you are living!

CHAPTER 17

THE RIGHT THING VS. THE EASY THING: ALWAYS PAY WHAT YOU OWE

MY DAD ALWAYS USED TO SAY, "BABY, it's not the easy thing, it's the right thing." That saying has blessed me so much in my life and businesses.

During my publishing days, I founded a set of magazines that became successful. I thoroughly enjoyed every (well, almost every) aspect of running them - the fashions, events, press coverage, red carpet interviews, awards shows, and spotlights were awe-inspiring! But of all my ventures, the magazine was the one venture that always ran in the red. No matter how well we were doing, there was always some area in which we needed to grow, and there went our earnings. We'd done various things to manage this that included growing and shrinking the number of writers, the type of submissions, the amount of words of the submissions, the compensation package, bringing the graphic department in-house, sending it back out, and a bit in-between, sending advertising out, bringing advertising in, and something in-between, bringing in more managers, decreasing managers . . . well, you get the point.

1. REMEMBER WHY YOU GOT STARTED.

No matter what was going on, I always made sure my people were paid. Sometimes it was a few days late, but always, always, always, they were paid. Even when it meant running up my credit cards, taking out two business lines of credit, and selling what I could release to the pawn shop. Seriously. Many people saw the posts and the magazine, and the videos, and the events and thought, "Wow, they are amazing! I wish I could be . . . (fill in the blank)." But the truth was that it was a lot of sacrifice and teamwork, empathy and compassion, challenge and tears, and struggle and pain that went into producing a magazine that didn't peddle in drama, exploiting other people's privacy and pain, nudity, or fear. We only highlighted people, organizations and causes that inspired us to live fearlessly. We had to fight harder for advertisers, harder for distribution, harder to get on the red carpet, and harder to sell out our shows. But God made a way for all of that and so much more. AND I had to ensure my team was protected – and part of that was ensuring they were compensated for work completed.

2. DO THE RIGHT THING, FOR THE RIGHT REASON, IN THE RIGHT WAY.

I remember one instance early in our journey when I hired one of our graphic designers to create a design for a client. My designer produced the work, but my client went with another design created by another graphic artist. I paid my designer anyway. He wrote me the most beautiful text, telling me how nobody else would have done that and that I would be blessed, indeed, because of it. To me, it was the right thing to do. Work was done and he needed to be paid. But for him, it was a huge show of loyalty because he'd been "had" before. What he didn't know was so "had" I. I know what it is to complete legal work for a client and he not pay because he's hitting the road to go to Mardi Gras. I know what it is to complete accounting work for a client and he not pay because he's in the middle of a pissing contest with someone in another department. I know what it is to serve as keynote of a program and bring down the house and the person responsible for paying me pays only a portion of what was agreed. I know what it is to babysit to earn extra money for our home as my mom worked two jobs to ensure we attended the best school and our clothes were on par with the other kids, only for the parent to decide that she's not going to pay what was agreed because she just doesn't feel like it . . . then call the following weekend for me to come back for round two. And I know what it is to work for a firm, coming in early, leaving late, teaching myself and going without a mentor because no one wanted to be bothered . . . while finding out that I was making $10K less than everyone else on my level. Yep, I'd "had" my share of being treated less than.

3. DECIDE YOU WILL BE BETTER AND DO IT.

I decided I was going to do more.

I decided that in spite of the craziness that we see on TV, my media would be a beacon of hope of what the world could be if we focused our minds to the wonder and wow of our divine creation.

I decided that I would give until there was nothing left, that when I leave this world it will be better for my presence in it and that people would know "I was here!" because THEY are better for me moving through their lives.

I decided that I would pay my people by any means necessary, even when it hurt (and sometimes it hurt a lot!).

Listening to my dad's words to do the right thing even when it's hard has helped me to avoid lapses in integrity that could have cost me my job, licenses, and reputation, in some instances. Those simple words have helped me to forge loyalty in my people that no money could ever buy, and they worked even when the money was late coming because they knew it WAS coming – come what may. That blessing my father covered me with at 18 as a freshman in college came because I wanted to move out of my apartment with three roommates because . . . well, it doesn't really matter. It would have left them in a bad way. That blessing had me hang in there long enough to ensure they were in a good place and we were able to remain friends.

Those nuggets of wisdom my father shared with me came from a time when he was a struggling college student, eating beans for a month because his "friends" didn't come through on a promise . . . but he had. His biggest regret wasn't that he'd kept his word that led to only having money for beans. Rather, his biggest regret was that he hadn't embraced who his "friends" were before that day and that it took such as a stark lesson for him to see and get to the truth. Hind sight is 20/20, but it can give you corrected lenses of wisdom of the same or better vision.

My dad finished dental school and one of the same "friends" didn't . . . because instead of holding to his word and doing what he said he'd do (studying and sharing knowledge with fellow colleagues), he goofed around and couldn't complete a procedure. My dad was no longer friends with this gentleman, so they were no longer hanging out and goofing off. My dad was focused and committed to his craft. And he moved home to Miami becoming the first African American orthodontist in Florida, the second in the South.

His dream was to ensure that African Americans received quality orthodontic care from a qualified practitioner. It was hard. A white orthodontist told him, "No nigger is ever going build a practice doing orthodontia."

4. ACCEPT HELP FROM PEOPLE POSITIONED TO HELP.

Ha. That white orthodontist hadn't met my godfather Dr. William Chapman.

My dad told his mentor, my godfather, what that man said, and he said "[Something unprintable], we'll show him!" And they did. They worked to build a referral network where the patients who came to the African American doctors were routed to my dad for braces. His business grew, and my dad never forgot why he started where he did. He was one of the first orthodontists to accept Medicaid (a big deal, because their fees were WAY below market and they were slow to pay), but these were the people he set out to serve. When he got tired and life got hard (divorce, a bad economy, death of his mentor, my godfather, and my grandmother's extended illness before passing really took a toll); he'd regroup and remind himself of why he got started. And then he'd ask himself about the right thing versus the easy thing.

5. WORK IN EXCELLENCE UNTIL YOU DECIDE ON THE NEXT THING.

The easy thing would have been to quit and live off social security. Instead, he worked until 80. The easy thing would have been to only serve those who could afford it. Instead, he always had a steady balance of pro bono cases (and taught me to do the same in every venture I've had – and it's been those thankful few who've been my loudest cheerleaders and paid client referrals!). The easy thing would have been to close the inner city office and only focus on the office in the affluent area. But when there were choices to be made, he kept the office in Liberty City (this was before the neighborhood revitalization project) and didn't leave until he retired at 80.

So, when I think about shutting it all down, I remember my dad's journey and think about his struggle to establish his dream of providing orthodontia for all, building such a practice on stubbornness and faith in his calling . . . And I dig in knowing that the apple didn't fall too far from the tree. I'm his daughter, his fiery strength and fortified blood charge through my veins. And I will continue to fight for human dignity, fight for empowered style, fight for loving relationships, give a voice to the community organizations aligned with my purpose, and be the leadership champion I was born to be.

Even when it hurts. And especially when it's not easy. Easy is ego. Easy is decreased opportunities to learn and grow one's AQ. Easy is one dimensional, flat, and linear - truly an "A to B" journey with no opportunities to grow or expand in one's overarching Being. The AQ hovers in limbo, waiting for the NEXT because there is nothing new offered or to be gained in the NOW.

Do the right thing.

Thanks Dad.

Blessings in the Lessons

1. Always pay what you owe. Pretending the debt doesn't exist doesn't serve you - that "pass" comes back in another form, only with you being the one hunting for your money.

2. Every venture is a success if you learned, grew, and prospered. Prosperity is fruitful gain - be it monetary or expansion in one's intellectual quotient(s). The former is the NOW manifestation of the latter, meaning if AQ increased then the bounty (material wealth) will as well, it just may take time. Be patient and have faith.

CHAPTER 18

TAKE OFF YOUR CAPE, NO ONE NEEDS TO BE SAVED

SOME TIME AGO, A FRIEND APPROACHED me about doing an event. I thought it was a cool idea and agreed to be a part of it. Emails were exchanged, a couple of phone calls were made, but nothing substantive came to pass. Then one day my friend called me frustrated because "nobody was doing anything". That hit a cord in me. I was emotionally hijacked - I know how it feels to feel alone, toiling on a project, and "nobody" does what they've said they would do. So, I took action. No, to be truly clear, I took over.

I called people in my network to rally behind the event. We secured the event planner, venue, set up the website and ticket portal, most of the entertainment, and coordinated the marketing. It was a success – total sell out, people left happy, and we received calls and requests asking when was the next one scheduled. And my friend was lost in the shuffle.

I have been incredibly fortunate, blessed really, to help people realize their dreams. Whether it's building a new business, discovering a new talent, or getting a project done that will help them advance to the next thing in their lives, I have had the opportunity to be a part of it and I loved every minute of it.

But that has also been an Achilles heel for me. I help people get things done that maybe shouldn't be done. Sometimes the wisdom and life experience that was supposed to be accomplished was the FAILURE of the project – and not the successful completion.

How can I say that? Because sometimes the greatest wisdom, empathy, and compassion for others comes from failure, disappointment, and regret. And those "negative" emotions can point a person to the answer or correct path that they'd been seeking and praying for . . . and your (or my) interference can delay that person's growth and advancement.

1. GIVE YOUR TIME, ATTENTION, AND GOOD ENVIRONMENT TO THE THING YOU WANT TO GROW.

AQ needs three things to grow strong, steady, and be firmly rooted: Time, attention, and good soil. The failure of a venture can provide all three that you will take to pause and lick your wounds, figure out what you did wrong and right; do things differently next time or not do "this" thing again at all.

Failure brings everything to a halt. Hard and immediate, it grabs your attention like success just doesn't. Even when you try to "walk it off" (the IT being hurt, humiliation, embarrassment, frustration, exasperation), you must give attention to the part of your mind that controls your emotions and decide to feel something different. Decisions demand attention.

The pause in all activity provides time for the lesson to take root in the soil (your soul) and grow into a blessing. The blessing of reevaluation, the gut check to verify that it was Christ Mind and not Yo' Mind (i.e., the ego) driving the endeavor. God can take questions. The Great I AM welcomes communication. It is in this time of silent stillness that you may commune with Him. Holy Spirit has the "floor", can speak and be heard uninterrupted. This is one of the few times the Big I can tell little i (ego) to go sit down in the corner and be quiet because the grownups are talking.

So, have the grown up convo. Ask for clear direction and listen to the answer. Seek clarification and find the path forward. Breathe. Just breathe and wait until you know what comes NEXT.

2. RECOGNIZE THE CIRCUMSTANCES THAT EMOTIONALLY COMPROMISE YOU, AND LEAVE YOUR CAPE IN THE DIRTY CLOTHES HAMPER.

I mentioned that my friend was lost in the shuffle as I "helped" her. How is that possible?

I heard her cry for help and I charged in to "save" her. She didn't need saving, she needed guidance and support. My efforts to save her were signs that I had unresolved "stuff" that needed attention, time and soil. In not recognizing that, I deprived my friend of a chance to grow.

Most of my friend's tribe, her supporters, left her hanging. Not one person she contacted came through as a sponsor. Not one person she asked to do preparation work did what they promised. Most of the people in attendance weren't from her circle. And although on the outside it looked fabulous, on the inside it was a stressful nightmare.

We worried up until the week of how we were going to pay for everything. I hit my sponsors to get it done – for a project that wasn't even mine and didn't really fit my platform – but they did it because they love and care about me.

We worried up until two weeks before what venue would host the event. Her tribal members who "had connections all over the city" weren't willing to use them for her.

We worried up until three weeks before who would serve on the panel of the event. The people who'd promised to serve as speakers went ghost and ignored all her calls, text messages, and emails.

4. BE A GOOD FRIEND AND LISTEN.

My friend was devastated. The 15 years prior to this event, she had served on literally dozens of boards and donated thousands of dollars and man hours serving various causes for and with these people who'd left her hanging. It was a painful moment to watch. And I wanted to "save" her from that pain because I'd been there, too. But I forgot the lesson that came from going through it and the wonder and the wow that followed. By interfering with the lesson, I prolonged that realization for HER.

I remember my first year serving as president of a prestigious women's organization. We planned a fundraiser that was to be THE fundraiser of the year. We secured the venue, printed tickets, identified speakers, circulated fliers and emails, and decorated everything black and silver. We were ready!

Nine people showed up. Including the speakers, we had 15 people total for an event that was supposed to host 100. That was one of the most embarrassing, painful, and expensive lessons I'd had up to that point. I was angry that my friends didn't support the event. I was angry the chapter didn't attend. I was angry the speakers didn't get anyone to come. I was angry, angry, angry! I was in my Ego, Ego, Ego!

And then the dust settled, and I was able to think. My AQ was able to grow because time, attention, and good soil were all present and ready to do their jobs.

I thought about the fact that WE didn't plan the event – I did. WE didn't secure the speakers – I did. WE didn't secure the venue – I did. There was no team – it was me, and only me, doing it all. And when there's an event of that magnitude that is supposed to help a group of people, then a group of people need to be together to get it done. And I learned. I understood. And I used that knowledge in my future endeavors. THAT was how I sold out events, built an award-winning media company with no PR background, established a publishing company with 7 bestselling authors with no publishing experience, and now consult with organizations around the world to develop their leaders although I have had all these flop experiences.

I forgot that it was the PAIN in the flop experience that brought me face-to-face with the raw truth of what was necessary to achieve that level of success. I interfered with my friend's opportunity to experience that glaring moment of honest, and she was never forced to embrace it because the event was executed successfully. Instead of getting my team in place to take over, I should have had the hard conversation with her about cancelling. Cancelling or postponing is not always an admission of failure, but rather an acknowledgment of unpreparedness – there is wisdom in seeing that.

Instead of securing the various parts of the event, I should have given her the information to do it herself, and just listened to her vent when things didn't go as planned. It's a real possibility that she would have been forced to get tough with her network and let them know that if they didn't come through for her, that they could forget about future support.

Instead of busting out my cape, I should have offered my shoulder to cry on and an ear to listen.

5. KNOW THAT IT MAY TAKE A TIME OR TWO TO GET THINGS RIGHT.

After that event, my friend went right back to donating money and serving on the boards of the same people who blew off her sponsor requests. She went back to overextending herself and twisting herself into a pretzel to help the same people who ignored her calls. And she started talking about Part Two before the weekend was over . . . and involving the same jokers who did nothing in the first place. The same dynamics that occurred the first time were already at play this second time around.

Except me.

I won't interfere this time.

I hate that I am going to watch my friend go through this. But I will be there to hold her hand, tell her it's going to be all right, and pick her up when it's over. Because I know the awesomeness that can and will be after transformation. Just like any great thing that comes in life, pain is a necessary part of it. I'm going to be there to help her transform her pain into HER ultimate gain.

I used to think harshly of people who stood by and watched people go through things. Not anymore because I now understand that they acknowledged the greatness within each person, the independence that exists in all women and men to make their own destinies. They understood what took me years to "get": I was born great, we each were. God gave each of us the ability to provide for ourselves when we departed Eden - "you will eat from the sweat of your brow" says Genesis. That means we were not helpless or without the connection with the Heavenly Father to do the impossible - we are INpossible - we are IN His will because we've asked God to "rest, rule, and abide in" us. That only happens when we decrease our ego and allow our AQ to provide a welcoming and receptive space for Divine Mind to operate.

So, all those people who refuse to be a part of our journey are still participating - they are bystanders at the parade. Spectators. Wave at them, thank them for coming, and keep right on marching. They understand your greatness - they came to see you - but they are not part of your production. And that's great - they don't know the routine anyway and would only mess it up. (Just like I did with my friend.)

6. BE PATIENT WITH YOURSELF; SOME THINGS WILL TAKE TIME TO TOTALLY SINK IN.

Know that some things are just "who you are": it's going to take a while for you to get all the parts of the Great Lesson.

I love hard working, dependable people. I work hard to surround myself with people like this, and most of the time, I succeed. One such person, who is always on her game, has a heart of gold, is an incredibly supportive person and a born leader. So, it was very unsettling the first time I experienced her do the opposite of everything that she said she would do. At first, I was very frustrated, and then it came to me during prayer one morning that she was operating out of her season.

We have a leadership nonprofit attached to our organization. It requires a lot of work to train women who are already established in their careers to make the jump into entrepreneurship and then finally into small business. My friend, and former graduate, wanted to volunteer and help with that process and I was more than delighted to accommodate her desire. Further, she had recruited two other graduates from her class to her help. I was ecstatic because I really didn't see how I was going to be able to do it by myself with the year that I knew I had coming up. And that was before I knew I was going to be moving out of state.

7. READ AND PAY ATTENTION TO THE TEA LEAVES.

Things started off great: She would check in with me, and we had meetings with her and the team, but then I noticed that nothing was being *done*. By the beginning of October, I knew that nothing was going to happen so I went into overdrive. I have gotten old enough to know that when things like this happen you don't get angry; you just get moving. You have a decision to make: Do you want to move forward with the thing that you have going (for me in this instance it was continuing our tradition of having a class graduate every year) or do you want to let the opportunity pass by (did I want to sit out a year)?

The answer to that was easy - I wanted to move forward. So, I made a way. For the first time our entire course was done using a video-based platform and it was done all in one day. Let me tell you it was probably one of the best and most effective courses we have ever had. For the class of people that we had who were all busy women needing everything condensed and recorded in a way that they could go back and review at their leisure, it was the best thing we could have ever done.

8. FORGIVE, THEN SEEK UNDERSTANDING.

After the class was over, my friend reached out to me and apologized for not doing what she said she would and asked if she could help. Of course I understood because sometimes I get overwhelmed and I'm not able to do what I said that I was going to do. I told her yes, and asked her to do the introductions during the graduation.

The day of the awards program came and I had already sent her the script, so it was just really a matter of reading. That didn't go as well as I thought it would. There was a little mix up with what was supposed to happen next which was strange because we had already discussed it. And then when it came to reading the script, well, she kind of went off and did her own thing. Normally that kind of thing would not have bothered me, but when it came time to introduce her honoree, she talked about how much she loved the person and how sweet the person was and how great the person was, but never mentioned the person's accomplishments and why she was being recognized. So, although *she* knew how great the lady was and *I* knew her great that sister was, *the audience* had no clue. All they saw was this one person receiving an award who my friend was saying was so great . . . but no reason why was every provided. It also looked strange because for every other person presented, the person doing the presentation read exactly what was on the paper - a summarized biography to let everybody know all of the great achievements that this person had accomplished and the community work they had done.

It was a real let-down. Enough so that I actually said something out loud which I don't do often. But I did this time. I voiced my frustrations to one of my best friends and to my husband. And it wasn't until later that I woke up one morning realized why I was so frustrated. I was not annoyed with my friend I was annoyed with myself.

I know what it looks like to work outside of your season. I know what it looks like to be tired and to try and push through anyway. And when I saw that friend was not doing what she said that she was going to do AT THE BEGINNING of this endeavor, I should have recognized the signs and told her no. I should have told her that I appreciated her reaching out and that I loved her, but I recognized that she needed rest. But I acquiesced because I did not want to hurt her feelings and I allowed her to stand up there and then create damage to herself and to her soul. That was not the right thing to do. The pain that I was experiencing was not frustration with my friend, who I recognized was in pain and piled onto her anyway. The frustration I had was with myself for even allowing that to happen.

I had invited my friend into my "Little Shop of Horrors". In the play and movie "The Little Shop of Horrors" Seymour has a little plant that only wants to eat blood. At first, it's just a little drink, but then as time goes on the little plant grows and demands even more blood. Eventually Seymour finds himself feeding the plant bodies to continue to grow his business. He becomes very successful and wealthy enough to take care of his family. It eventually compromises his morality and ultimately requires the sacrifice of everything that he has worked for.

As an entrepreneur and business owner I sympathize with Seymour. We start businesses initially with just a drop of blood. And we continue to give and give and give until there is nothing else that we personally can do, and then we start to give even more and more and more until it has compromised our health and our family structure. So, when I say I knew what my friend was going through, this is not some trite statement or condescendingly egotistical proclamation. I felt it in my soul.

9. BE TRANSPARENT IN LOVE.

And it meant that I knew how to help, and I did. I shared with my friend the importance of staying focused on why she got started on her life path in the first place.

All the trappings of success and wealth had to go if it was compromising her ability to enjoy them. No one goes into business to feed a greedy little plant. It is to help others (i.e., solve a problem) and generate income to take care of ourselves and the people we love. Anything that gets in the way of those things has to go – even if it means letting people down, breaking commitments, and generally going missing for a time.

Beloved, the world is billions of years old, and it will live another billion. It was fine before you, is fine now, and will be fine long after you are gone. Therefore, if you sit down and rest a month or two or three, the world will still turn. People will miss you, but they will adjust. And when you are ready to get back into the swing of things, either those people will welcome you with open arms or not. Either way, you are going to be all right. Totally, completely all right. And so, will they be.

Blessings in the Lessons

1. AQ requires time, attention, and good soil to grow. Failure provides all those things.
2. Well-meaning friends can sometimes impede our efforts to realize the awe-inspiring person Creative Intelligence designed us to be.
3. Our spec-porters (spectator supporters) provide the rain to water our soil. Embrace them with joy.

CHAPTER 19

INFORMATION ABOUT A THING PROVIDES CHOICE IN ACTION; KNOWLEDGE OF A THING REQUIRES ACTION

DOMESTIC VIOLENCE IS A DEVASTATING consequence of unrelenting pain.

I found out that a person with whom I have been having a private war for years was the victim of spousal abuse. I didn't know because the abuse was not physical (to the best of my knowledge). I say "to the best of my knowledge" because anyone with sense knows that victims of domestic violence are very adept at hiding their physical bruises. And the mental and emotional abuse many times can be much more traumatic than the physical ever could be.

1. TAKE IN THE INFORMATION, BUT NOT THE EMOTION.

I found out that this person who I'm supposed to love had been suffering at the hands of a brute for 35 years. This person is significantly older than I, and I didn't know that that's what was going on. I offer no excuse other than to say that many times when we know people from our childhood and we grow up, they never really age or grow old in our minds because we continue to view them through our child-like eyes.

But I am not a child.

I have worked with victims of domestic abuse as a volunteer, as an advocate, and as an attorney. I know the signs and the fact that I totally missed it and attributed this person's behavior to just being a mean (fill in the blank) is inexcusable.

2. ALLOW THE INFORMATION TO DEEPEN INTO KNOWLEDGE.

What's even deeper than that is my behavior would have been different had I known that she was being abused, but the truth is it shouldn't have made any difference.

I know when people are acting out and saying inappropriate things that it is indicative of pain.

A person lashing out is the equivalent of a deep wound on your arm. It's an outward sign of trauma and a cry for help. It is a symptom of something else that needs to be addressed. An examination needs to be completed. There needs to be antibiotics or alcohol applied, and an assessment on whether a bandage is needed or even stitches or surgery.

Not just cursing somebody out and walking away. The wound is still bleeding.

Not just turning your back on the person and pretending like they don't exist. The wound still needs attention.

Not embarrassing them in front of your circle. The wound will get infected and lead to more trauma.

Getting to the heart of an issue requires sitting down and trying to figure out what's going on; and how you can help and love that person better.

3. EVALUATE WHAT YOU CAN DO TO IMPROVE THE SITUATION.

I was able to change course with my behavior because that person needed me to rise up and be better. I was able to help dress the wound because I wanted to stand tall and BE better. But I tell you the truth: it would have been more comfortable to ignore the calls to do something.

The ego is self-centered. Its main job is to stay in charge. Therefore, it knows exactly what obligations will remove it from power. Laying down arms and brokering peace is one of those actions. But the ego puts forth maximum effort in presenting cohesive arguments to dissuade you from doing so. And if you've ever tried to help a drowning person or wounded animal, you know that in their pain and panic, they will lash out at you. They will thrash about so strongly that if you don't handle the situation with care, you may be wounded – sometimes mortally.

My ego made that argument and I moved to help anyway.

I was inconvenienced when I rose to help. I missed an entire day of work. When you work for yourself, you feel the pain of missing a day.

My ego hit me where it hurt - my pocket. I moved forward anyway.

I worked without getting paid. I created legal documents to protect her and ran interference against people who would have kept her in that situation for their own purposes. It had been a while since I'd last served in such capacity. I'd forgotten how invigorating holding the shield of faith could be . . . and how heavy it could get. I needed to work out!

My ego didn't like that at all. My getting stronger meant that my AQ was making room for the Christ in Me to reign on the throne.

I am very grateful that the opportunity for me to rectify my behavior did not pass me by. I had an opportunity to help this person who is now suffering from early onset dementia. But I will not allow myself to forget this incredible lesson. When people act out it's a cry for help and it is not okay to reciprocate in kind.

Blessings from the Lessons

1. Life is a peace kingdom, not a battle field. If we want to grow into the person who can rule it well, then we must disarm our "troops" (ego) and reinstall the Rightful Ruler.

2. You've got to give to get. Sacrificing the NOW satisfaction of being right leads to the NEXT luxury of being in love.

CHAPTER 20

HOW TO PREPARE FOR THE UNEXPECTED "NO YOU DID NOT JUST . . . !"

A S AN ATTORNEY, I HAVE COMPLETED a ton of real estate closings (paper is still coursing out of my ears). One of the lenders I work with frequently has a wonderful policy of sending documents to the client for review at least two days prior to closing. They call the client to review the numbers and answer any questions they may have the day prior to closing. When this lender's clients sit down with me, they are ready to sign . . . except in this one instance.

Mr. and Mrs. Jones (names have been changed) received their documents three days prior to the closing via overnight mail. Mr. Jones was traveling and did not have the opportunity to review the paperwork. Mrs. Jones received the package but did not review it. She took the call from the lender's representative but did not ask any questions - she decided to wait until it was time to sign on the dotted line.

1. KNOW THAT NO MATTER HOW MUCH YOU PLAN, PEOPLE DO WHAT THEY WANT TO DO.

When we sat down at the table, Mrs. Jones took out a pocket calculator and started to check the numbers. Her husband looked at her in astonishment and shouted, "What are you doing?!" She giggled nervously that she wanted to make sure everything was correct. He told her that she should have done that before and that she needed to sign - now. They argued for a few minutes, and finally she relented and they signed. I was embarrassed for both of them.

The disrespect both displayed in front of a stranger was unreal. Mrs. Jones should have reviewed all information prior to the closing and trying to recalculate the information was a bit over the top. But Mr. Jones could have communicated with her in a more diplomatic way (i.e., without yelling) and in private to convey his displeasure. I had never witnessed anything like that before, so I sat there stunned like a deer in headlights. The embarrassment was so acute that I felt heat come up my back and into my hairline. I remembered thanking God for my chocolate complexion because the blush I felt could not be seen! And yet . . .

2. SHOW SOME EMOTION.

As I look back at that moment, I realize that maybe it would have been good to communicate what I really felt in those moments. It would have been a good thing if Mr. Jones had seen that I was not stoic, I was mortified. It would have been good if Mrs. Jones had seen that I was not smug, but deeply uncomfortable. And it would have been good if I had not pretended all was well, because it wasn't.

The lack of affection between them was sad. Mr. Jones had no sympathy for the reasons Mrs. Jones put forth as to why she had not reviewed the paperwork. In his mind, she was a housewife, and had plenty of time to get the business taken care of. It didn't seem to occur to him that in raising four children and managing their household that she could be pressed for time. In his mind, he made the bacon and it was her responsibility to make it edible - by any means necessary.

Mrs. Jones had no sympathy for Mr. Jones' jet lag or my time. In her mind, he had a cushy job as an executive and flew first class from London, so he could not be too tired. It did not occur to her that after being on a plane and in airports for more than half a day that he would be tired. Nor that I had other appointments with people who had taken the time to review their documentation prior.

I don't consider myself a referee, marriage counselor,

or therapist, but I do know God places us in situations to learn, grow, and influence people. You have to be authentic to do those things, and I wasn't. I missed the opportunity for all of the above by sitting there admiring my nail polish.

It took a few years to get the above three sentences together, but when I did, I promised myself that when my "No You Did Not Just . . ." moment came, I would rise to the occasion like cream in coffee. And I knew it wouldn't take long because every day I meet the most interesting people.

A few weeks later, the opportunity presented itself in the form of Margaret (name has been changed). She was a very pretty woman, in her late thirties, ultra-feminine, and everything in her home was pink, green, or cream.

When I arrived at Margaret's home, she greeted me warmly, offered me refreshments on fine china, and we conducted our business in her parlor. About half way through the paperwork, Margaret's husband came into the room and voiced his displeasure about the transaction. Margaret had purchased her home prior to the marriage and had never added her husband to the deed nor to the mortgage (that's a discussion for another time). The mortgage was 10 years from being paid in full, and Margaret was taking out $30,000 from the equity to get plastic surgery.

I was floored. I knew she was taking out equity during

the transaction, but I did not know why (it was none of my business). But I could not help but ask her why. She explained that I was still young and did not understand what older women went through. She gently cradled my face in her hands, depressing my cheeks, and said, "See, your cheeks are still full, your lips still plump." She then touched her own face, which was beautiful - a little gaunt, but still well defined - and said, "My cheeks are no longer full and I no longer look young."

I told Margaret that I thought she was beautiful. She smiled sadly but said in a determined voice that I sounded like her husband. He did not want her to have the surgery. He believed they should pay off the house and retire comfortably in their late forties, but since he was not an owner on the property, he did not have a legal right to stop her.

When I dug a bit deeper, Margaret told me that they had had a huge argument prior to my arrival, and that she had said to him, "You are plain, and your people are plain! My family is beautiful. You don't understand!"

Wow.

We finished our business and she wished me well. I was so taken aback by the entire encounter, I stepped out of "professional" mode and told her that I would be praying for her speedy recovery.

When I got home, I went straight to my husband and just hugged him tight. He asked me what was wrong, and I told him about my day. He could not believe what I was saying. (Actually, he did believe it - I have stories like this in droves - but this one was a bit out there.) I told my husband that I loved him very much, that I thought he was very handsome, and promised I would never talk to him like that. He laughed heartily. I was incensed because I thought we were having a sweet moment. He placed his hands on my shoulders before I could get worked up and told me that he was laughing because he knew I would never talk to him like that, and the thought of it was so ridiculous there was nothing to do but laugh. My husband's AQ is very high and has been since we met in college. He doesn't allow much to get under his skin and chooses to see the humor in most situations. It's a great way to ensure his spiritual growth is not stymied by perceived slights and imagined drama.

That night before going to bed, I reviewed my time with Margaret. There were so many variables at play in that situation, but they all come back to one main culprit – pain.

Physical beauty has an outlying importance in our society, so much so, that people forget that spiritual beauty always overrides the physical. The act of forgetting leads to the acts of cruelty, disrespect, and sometimes, absolute chaos.

When Margaret told me about her argument with her "plain" husband, she made no effort to lower her voice so he would not hear. It was awful to tell him that she thought he was plain looking, and that his entire family were plain people; and absolutely terrible to repeat to me - a stranger! - within his earshot.

But that's what pain does – it deafens us to common decency. It numbs us to common care. It obliterates all reason. It flushes our every "Q" - IQ, EQ, SQ, AQ - down the toilet.

But we can come back from it. We can hear again, feel again, and be made whole again. How? By owning it. Our AQ demands all parts of our psyche to be fully engaged and the only way that occurs is if we take responsibility for our thoughts, feelings, and actions. That is the very definition of ownership.

We have to face facts – we were hurt. We must be honest – we felt bad. We must press forward – we know there's better on the other side.

Margaret was still a beautiful woman. Period. Not "beautiful for an older woman", not "beautiful in spite of those wrinkles", she was "BEAUTIFUL" PERIOD.

But it hurt to hear those qualifying statements for the first time in her life.

And it hurt to see fewer heads turn as she walked by.

Once Margaret admits the hurt, then it will hurt less. One day it'll hurt less when she doesn't hear the compliments nor see the heads not turn because she won't care. Her spiritual beauty will radiate so powerfully that nothing will be comparable to it.

We have choices in this life. We may choose to be pummeled by life and give up, or fight back and keep swinging until we win. We may allow someone else's definitions of beauty, success, and happiness rule us or we will create our own and live boldly and fearlessly with all the "wonder" and "wow" God created within us on full display.

We can choose to use each encounter as opportunities - blessings from the Great I Am - to grow our AQ; or we may devolve into pieces every time someone needles us on some superfluous quality (you're fat, you're ugly, you're not one of "us", you're black, you're white, you're old, you're young, you're straight, you're gay, you're . . . YOU).

Raise your personal bar, and leap over it. You are not leaving anyone behind, rather, you're leading those who want out of the mental oppression to the Promised Land. Embrace the pain and watch the blessings reign.

No one's opinion matters but yours so be sure to give your "matter" quality substance. Sometimes the lesson must be presented repeatedly until we get it right so we may move on to the NEXT, i.e., the next great life adventure. Sometimes that adventure is understanding that your bodily functions take precedence over all else.

I don't mind meeting my clients wherever is most convenient for them - my office, their office, or their homes. I like the flexibility to run errands, do lunch with friends and colleagues, and generally get out into the fresh air during daylight hours. But when traffic is bad and/or I run late to appointments, things could get pretty hairy.

I laughed with a colleague that sometimes we would put off our bodily functions for the sake of being on time, only to get a client that has an issue or wants to question every word, making an appointment that should have been 30 minutes, tops, last two hours. This colleague said to me that she once almost lost her bladder three times in one day because she did not want to stop to use the restroom for fear of being tardy. Fear will make you lose your mind and your dignity.

I sympathized in that I, too, had been faced with the challenge, but for the most part, I was comfortable using my client's restroom if it came down to it. Until the unthinkable happened. I had to use the restroom, I thought it would be quick, but it was not. The water pressure at the client's home was so low, it took three flushes (and several minutes between) to clear the commode. I was embarrassed to the roots of my hair. I emerged from the powder room with as much dignity as I could muster and completed the transaction. I shared the experience with my colleague and listened to her laugh so hard she could not breathe.

Although glad I could offer her such entertainment (said with heavy sarcasm), I learned a valuable lesson that day. My bladder is more important. Others can wait while you do what you need to do. It is a natural occurrence and they will not die to wait.

And as life would have it, my opportunity to apply this valuable lesson came not too long after. I like starting my programs on time. Whether it is a graduation for our non-profit, the Jewell Jackson McCabe Emerging Leaders Institute, or our annual leadership awards program, the BOLD Lifestyles Awards, it is my goal to start and end according to the program. But, sometimes being late is not only unavoidable, it's preferable to the alternative of complete disaster.

Not too long ago, we hosted our annual BOLD Lifestyles Awards program and we were running late. Really late. Really, really late. And I was furious. I had done everything I could to ensure we would start and end on time - carefully scripted programs, prepared honorees, hired a world-class planner and five assistants, engaged an award-winning caterer, secured professional entertainers, and completed pre-sales. And yet I did not count on the one thing that no one on this earth has any control over - the weather. I did not account for the incredible storm system that covered over 200 miles of the area that included the venue where my attendees would be traveling to attend. There were tornados, flooding, and torrential thunder and lightning storms everywhere. It was horrible!

But do you know 300 people still came?! Yet, I was

focused on the fact that we started 45 minutes late, had to switch the lineup because people were trying to get to the conference center through the storm, and that some people were not their absolute best because they were a bit rattled due to the weather. Just like I had to fight through that storm, so did other people. Two people's cars broke down - one called an Uber and the other hopped a ride to the airport to rent a car. Outfits were ruined due to the mud. Food deliveries did not make it fully intact. Equipment was damaged. But everybody showed up and pushed forward anyway, just to be in the place. Because they wanted to be there for me.

In my singular focus to be timely, I once again forgot my bladder was more important. My bladder in this instance was the PEOPLE. It took two days for me to remember. Two days of holding my bladder. Two days of stewing on being late, focused on the fact that we went over time – even though the venue did not even charge us for it. But on the third day, I remembered. I re-membered. I got my mind right and rejoined the land of the reasonable and released my grievances so I could say "Thank you". My AQ was allowed to ascend in gratitude and thankfulness. And I said "Thank you".

Thank you for fighting through the weather. Thank you for staying as long as you could to enjoy the program. Thank you for folding your dress over to hide the stain instead of going home and giving up. Thank you for smiling politely and not going off when the food ran out. Thank you for agreeing to swap sets so everyone could perform and earn their pay. Thank you for not holding out so I did not have an accident and wet myself in front of the whole world.

Some lessons have to be presented multiple times before we get them. Thankfully, we worship a mighty understanding God who doesn't mind and is with us every step of the way.

Blessings from the Lessons

1. Own your feelings. You will not move on to the next great adventure successfully until you master the one in front of you.
2. Face your fears and remember you come first. Once your own needs are met, you will be able to provide exceptional attention and care to those around you.
3. Express gratitude to your family, friends, colleagues, and neighbors. When you see all that you have to be grateful for, you'll be able to move quickly past the petty and see the beauty behind it.

CHAPTER 21

SOME PROTECTIONS COME IN THE FORM OF "PUNISHMENT"

ONE NIGHT I STOPPED TO GET GAS AND while I was at the pump, I heard a loud noise like a car hitting something. I looked out into the street. A car had hit the curb so hard that it blew the tire. The driver was able to maneuver the car into the gas station, and when she surveyed the damage, not only was the tire blown, the rim was also bent.

Both the driver and the passenger had gotten out of the car to assess the situation, and when the passenger saw the bent rim, she began to swear - I mean really salty language. The driver was stoic and I couldn't understand how she maintained such an unmoved demeanor until she began to speak. She was so drunk she was desensitized. The words indicated that there should have been some emotion behind them, but she was so drunk she could not communicate any emotion. The passenger had had a few as well because I could smell it on both of them, but she was nowhere near as drunk as the person who had been driving. After trying to convince the owner of the car that the damage was not as bad as she thought, they tried to change the tire without success.

I made sure that they were all right (and also to ensure that they would not be able to get back on the road). I thought about what I had seen on my way home and I couldn't understand why I was placed in that situation to observe it even though I could do nothing about it. And then it came to me.

There are times in our lives when we experience a setback, it seems to come out of nowhere, and we can't understand why. But I can tell you that it is protective. Protective pain is a circumstance that arises that causes you great angst, consternation, and sometimes bitterness in the moment. But, in the overall theme, saves you from a fate that could have resulted in grave injury to yourself and/or someone you care for.

Sometimes we pray huge prayers and ask for things without adding "according to thy will". Our prayers don't just cover us, but they cover those around us as well. When we pray, we're not only praying that we are not hurt, but also that we don't hurt others. Well, that driver was drunk and her bending that rim prevented her from getting back on the road was protection – for her and everyone else on the road.

Follow me now. She gave the keys to her car, the way that she manages to get to work every day, to someone who was so drunk that they could not drive in a straight line. That driver could have killed herself, the owner of the car and everybody else on the road that night. But she didn't. Instead she just hit the curb and blew a tire, causing them to pull over. I bet it will be a long time before the owner of that car ever allows another person that drunk to drive her car again.

Sometimes protective pain is financial because that is a pain that we are very slow to forget. Don't believe me? Follow this. When someone borrows money from you and they don't pay you back, are you so quick to give them another loan? Of course not. When you take a job and they don't pay you what they're supposed to, the next time you interview aren't you more diligent to ensure your paycheck says exactly what it's supposed to? Of course, you do.

So now I'm looking at this situation where this woman was going to have to have her car towed on a flatbed (and if she could not afford to do it voluntarily, it was going to be towed and impounded). She has to pay the tow fee and the redemption fee prior to the tow company selling the car (because you know that they can do that if you don't come get the car in a certain period of time, right?). Then she has to have the car towed to a repair shop to repair the rim and then the tire. All of this is easily going to cost between

$800 to $1,000 when it's all said and done. Do you think after an experience like that the owner of that car is going to have somebody drunk driving her car again?

We don't like protective pain because it hurts, but sometimes it's the answer to an unspoken prayer. And it can also be a motivator to look within and grow. If things in your life are not going right, it is time to turn your gaze inward.

1. LOOK IN THE MIRROR AND GAZE UPON THYSELF.

I used to work with a young lady who was incredibly bright, truly a shining star. I knew and still know without a shadow of a doubt that she is going to be a powerhouse once she grows into her full potential. The problem is that right now she's going through something. She tends to work within an organization for about a year to year-and-a-half, learn everything she can and take those ideas and thoughts that she gained and use them in other people's organizations. Of course, I did not realize that's what she was doing until she did it to me and my organization.

I never said anything to her about it and it was very interesting to me when one day she called me out of the blue totally depressed. She said, "I don't know what to do next in my life! I don't understand why things are not happening for me." And my response to her was, "If you really want to know the answer to that question, then pray and ask the Lord and He will answer you."

I think she heard in my voice that I knew why things weren't working out and that she had been found out because I never heard back from her. I wish I had charged in and told her what was on my mind. I did not because I did not feel she would receive it. But that does not absolve me of the responsibility to do it. She called, and I did not answer. I could give a number of reasons, but they are all simply excuses, and excuses are impediments to elevation, manifestation, and expansion - AKA moving up in the world.

2. YOU CAN'T MOVE UP UNTIL YOU LEARN TO SPEAK UP.

I pray big prayers because I dream big dreams. It's not that I don't get scared; some days, I would shake in my boots wondering how things were going to come together. But the one thing I've learned in all that fear is that unless or until I open my mouth, nothing is going to get done.

Or as Mom used to say, "Closed mouths don't get fed."

A colleague of mine learned that lesson and it really blessed her in an unexpected way. I'd asked her to do a task that included interviewing people for one of my clients. She and my client were friendly, so she was happy to do it. And she did it very well. My colleague arrived early, was enthusiastic, very professional, and made each subject feel special. (I knew she would, that's why I asked her to do it.)

The problem came when my client failed to thank her. It's one of those things: if you thank no one, you're okay, if you do a general "thanks everyone", you're okay, but if you thank everyone but forget one person, you're toast. Well, my colleague was the one left behind and it was not pretty.

She was stunned. After leaving work early, rescheduling a doctor's appointment, battling afternoon traffic, rushing home to change and grab equipment, and doing a phenomenal job for almost five hours (when it was supposed to be three hours), no "thank you" came from the stage. I had no idea that occurred because I was in and out of the room working, so I just assumed that all thank yous took place while I was out (hmmm, you know what they say about assuming . . .).

Not knowing what all took place, I called my associate on the way home to thank her for the phenomenal job she did. She sounded sad and I commented on it. She said she was just tired, but I know her well – I know her tired voice, and that was not it. She sounded sad, so I pressed her. And she erupted.

O. M. G. She was no longer stunned. She was MAD.

She couldn't believe that after all she'd gone through to be there and make the interviews special, that the only "thank you" that came was after the program was over...

and my client looked at her and realized she had left her behind.

I sat quietly and listened. When she was done, I asked if she was going to say anything. Initially, she said no – she wanted to put it behind her. I was quiet. (She knows that my silence speaks volumes.) She asked what I thought, so I told her she should say something.

Before I finish this story, I must pause to say that it's important to speak up for yourself when YOU are ready to say something, not when someone else says (or intimates) that you should. Your life experience is about you, and if you only move when pushed to do so, and it's not of your own volition, then your AQ does not have the opportunity to grow . . . and you will encounter the same situation (with different players) over and over again until you get the lesson. This is not punishment, but preparation for the things YOU prayed for. Your hopes and dreams require certain levels of power and skill, so as they become bigger and grander, so too, will the experiences that "come" (i.e. you bring) into your life to prepare you to actually enjoy the fruits of your labor.

Also, you want to be sure you voice the FACTS and your feelings about the FACTS. You also want to ensure that you say everything you need to say so you may leave it all behind you.

Now, back to the story.

My colleague equivocated, so I let it rest and we moved on to something else.

A couple of days later, my client called to tell me she'd heard from my associate. She'd sent an email detailing from start to finish her feelings and everything she went through (including leaving work early) to make things work. My client felt terrible and apologized profusely. But she also called me to get ideas on what could be done to make it up to her. And we came up with a few pretty awesome conciliatory offers that my colleague absolutely loved.

But none of that would have been possible if she had not spoken up for herself.

Yes, it was painful recounting what she felt. Yes, it was uncomfortable talking it through. Yes, there was a chance that the conversation might have gone sideways. But if you're not willing to take the chance to push past pain and get to the other side of it, you'll never even have the opportunity for something better, or something more, than what you have now. If you're good with what you have, then fine. Let it rest. But you wouldn't be reading this book if you really believed that.

My client also learned a valuable lesson – either do one general "Thank You" to everyone for their hard work or make a list and refer to your notes so you do not forget anyone. As my mom would say, "Ninety percent of execution is in the planning," or "Failing to plan is planning to fail," as they say in the armed forces.

3. KNOW WHEN SILENCE IS THE BEST ACTION.

But there are times when you are called, and you are not supposed to answer. There are some people in this world who have helped you so much and bless your life in such a way that even when you are no longer as close as you once were (or possibly don't speak at all), you still protect them and shield them because the affection you have for them does not go away. You just tuck it away deep inside of your heart, away from the world.

I had an experience years ago where a mentor, who was a huge part of my life and in me becoming the woman I am today, referred me to work with one of her colleagues. This person was a well-known author, highly accomplished and recognized all over the world and I was deeply honored.

My mentor and I had grown apart through the years, but she had never forgotten me and I really appreciated that. When I was on the phone with her colleague and she asked me very casually how I knew my mentor, I rained down Love Fest for my mentor all over that woman. I gushed about all that she had done for me, and how much I loved her. And I ended it by saying that I would not be the woman I am today without her.

Her colleague quickly ended the call. I was a little taken aback because I could not understand what I said that would result in the call ending so quickly. It was not until much later in life that I understood. It was jealousy. Sometimes when we get to places in our lives, our colleagues become friends but they still have flaws and some of them fatal. One of those flaws is jealousy. It's not that they don't want you to do well, it's that they don't want you to do better than they do. And when you get older, part of your success is your legacy, one in which you pray the Next Generation heralds sing your laurels.

So here I am talking about how wonderful this woman was to me and her colleague was literally shutting it down. Shutting me out. Shutting her out. It was very sad. I never told my mentor what happened because I felt that it would hurt her, nor did I want to get into a game of "he said, she said" (my mother always said, "Watch the dog who carries the bone," when it came to gossip and conjecture, and I am not a dog). But I never forgot that lesson and so when people in my life act a little funny, I don't get angry - I understand that it is jealousy. Jealousy because they feel that they have not done everything they could have and should have done to get where they believe they should be. Not understanding that in every moment of their lives they are where they want to be and that every moment of their lives they have the opportunity to be everything they ever wanted to be!

God gave each of us our own gifts, skills, and opportunities to shine. There is no reason to try to take other people's spotlight. There is no time to be a mini-me – embrace the big, brilliant YOU.

If things are not going right in your life, it is not always someone else - it really could be you. Take time to look at yourself and take stock. Sometimes you are what is standing in your way. But how can you discern the good from the bad? I'll tell you . . . by surrounding yourself with good people who will tell you.

But how do you know when you have something special? Well, if you're hanging around the right people you'll find out soon enough. When you and the person you're in a relationship with have an argument and you are being irrational and talking about breaking up, if you are with a good person and you're hanging around the right people, those people are going to fight for your relationship. Why? Because they love you. They're going to tell you when you are being a bonehead, when you need to apologize or stand your ground. They are going to help you get to where you want to be in a way that honors who you are. The "relationship" in this scenario can be romantic, professional, or filial.

After all of those experiences, I finally learned when and how to unleash in my "no you did not just do . . ." moment. My husband left the lights on in his car one night when it was 22 degrees outside. I was the last to arrive home, about 8pm, when I noticed the lights on in my husband's car. I thought maybe he was unloading, and still needed to make another trip, so I sent my daughter down to the basement to see what state of dress he was in. (When my husband puts on his favorite collegiate tee shirt and matching shorts, the day is done.) Sure enough, my daughter reported that daddy was indeed attired in his "the day is complete" attire. I went down to tell him his lights were on, but he met me at the top of the stairs. Once he understood the situation, he picked up his keys and headed toward the garage . . . and outside . . . in the 22-degree cold . . . with no shoes on.

The native Miamian in me rose up and said in an incredulous voice, "You are NOT going outside without any shoes on! Babe, it's freezing out there!" My hubby tilted his head to the side, nodded, and went downstairs to put on shoes. When he came back in, he smiled a bit sheepishly at me and said, "Mission accomplished." We laughed and went downstairs to watch a movie.

Spouses don't mind being fussed over; they mind being fussed AT. My guy knew it was cold, and if anyone else in our house had tried to do that, he would have said something, too. Although born and raised in Michigan, he knows he is not impervious to cold . . . most days. And although my voice was sharp, my babe knew it was because I cared about his health and general welfare. If I had not said anything, he would have thought something was wrong.

People can tell you they love you all day long, but the showing is where the rubber hits the road. The showing requires us to be vulnerable and open to being rejected, rebuked, and embarrassed, but it's always worth the risk. No risk, no reward. No pain, no gain.

Blessings in the Lessons

1. Love and respect go hand in hand. You can convey disapproval of an action in a kind manner. And if you can't think of a way to do so respectfully, then hold the thought until you can.

2. Protection sometimes takes the form of punishment. Don't take it personally - it happens to all of us. After you've cooled your jets, review your actions and see what and why things transpired in the manner in which they did. Accept the answer and take appropriate action.

3. Surround yourself with good people in every area of your life and listen to them. They love you, have their own success patterns to enjoy, so have no reason to be jealous or envious of you. Thank them often and pray for them daily.

CHAPTER 22

THINK. MAYBE SPEAK. ALWAYS ACT IN ACCORDANCE WITH YOUR HIGHEST THOUGHT.

I SERVE A NUMBER OF SENIOR CITIZENS IN my law practice and would often go to their homes to save them the hassle of traveling around the city (traffic could be absolutely crazy some days). I usually confirm my appointments a few days before, just to ensure my clients are still available to conduct business. Upon such an occasion, I placed a call to a senior citizen named Mrs. Monroe (name changed). The phone was disconnected. I tried again, just in case I had misdialed with the same result. I tried the next day, but the number was still out of service.

On the day of the appointment, I called the number and gratefully, it was working. I introduced myself to Mrs. Monroe, and let her know I would be at her home at the appointed time. I also informed her of the requirements to complete the transaction. She was not prepared (unfortunately, that was not a surprise - that was one of the reasons I wanted to confirm the appointment). Mrs. Monroe was very upset that she did not have all the documentation that would be required to complete her transaction and began to berate me for not calling her in advance. I stopped her mid-tirade and explained that I had called, but her phone was out of order. (I did not say it was disconnected because I did not want to embarrass her. As I had the very intimate details of her financial situation, I knew that she was living "close to the line" and that every penny in her household was accounted for and already spent before it was received.)

Mrs. Monroe was indignant and blustered that I had to have called the wrong number, nothing was wrong with her phone, and I should have notified her of these requirements before the day of the appointment. I tried again to explain that I had dialed her number, but that the call did not go through. Before I could finish, she raised her voice, spoke over me, and told me that I had dialed the wrong number. I paused and took a deep breath, counting to ten, then to fifteen. I believe Mrs. Monroe sensed my frustration and knew that she had crossed the line - she had just called me a liar and I still needed to complete her business.

No fool, Mrs. Monroe changed tactics, asking me if I

had directions and letting me know that she would have all required documents. I thanked her and ended the call.

When I arrived, Mrs. Monroe was sweet as pie. We completed our business without incident and I left. As I reflected on that situation, I saw the pain, but also the gain.

There are times when you just have to let it go. Mrs. Monroe was in a bad way financially, and she was stressed mentally, which compromised her emotional state. I believe that Mrs. Monroe was a kind woman who would only abandon courtesy under extreme duress. Accusing a stranger of lying about calling her home when she knew her phone had been disconnected, probably because she had not paid the bill, is nonsensical. But it is something someone would do if embarrassed and stressed. They are also powerful opponents to self-improvement. They unhinge our sense of reason (IQ), obliterate common courtesy (EQ), obscure the "Christ in Me" (SQ) and thereby decimate our AQ (the sum of all of these components).

Stress and embarrassment are two of the most forceful pain triggers. Relieving pressure by allowing things to pass without comment or reference are sure ways to calm things down quickly.

Of course I was offended by Mrs. Monroe's accusation that I had lied about calling. I had no reason to do so, and every reason to want her to have all the documentation she needed - without it, we could not complete the transaction and I would not be paid. But when I considered it from the perspective that Mrs. Monroe would have done and said the same thing to any person who called, I relaxed a bit. Although what she said was personal to me in that she said to me, it was not to be taken personally because Mrs. Monroe would have said that to anyone standing in my shoes. Add that to the fact that Mrs. Monroe did her best to make amends when I came to her home - she had refreshments prepared on her "good" china and crystal goblets to drink our water. She had done her best to apologize without saying the words.

Here's a secret: The words aren't really that important. Truth is, when people hurt us, we want them to stop AND we want it to never happen again. No one likes the person who apologizes yet continues to do the same thing over and over again. So, the fact that Mrs. Monroe never apologized verbally, but did so through warm hospitality and kindness upon my arrival was the best and most genuine apology.

By taking the time to focus on the task at hand - getting the business done; and seeing things from her perspective, I was able to release the offense I had taken. To be offended, you have to take it. If you do not acknowledge or accept bad behavior as a reflection upon you, then it isn't. If you don't shout back when someone is trying to pick a fight, then there is no argument (remember, "it takes two to tango"). If you let the pain recede from your heart, mind, and soul like waves rolling back into the ocean then the gain is revealed as the sand on the beach.

Your life is your creation, gifted to you by Divine Mind to do with as you please. So, live in pleasure. Be pleased by who you meet and what you do. Indulge in the pleasantries of community. And embrace the pleasing nature of God in you.

Blessings in the Lessons

1. Focus on the raison d'etre, which is the business at hand. That focus allows you to quickly move past feelings of offense and later dissect the "hows" and the "whys" to get to the blessings of a situation.

2. Respect the elderly. One day you will be where they are and the world may look a bit differently to you when many of your friends have passed away, the places you used to frequent have closed or changed, and nothing you used to enjoy comes on television any longer.

CHAPTER 23

MAN CLEAN: DOES YOUR ENVIRONMENT REFLECT YOUR PRESENCE, I.E., DOES IT LOOK LIKE YOU LIVE HERE?

I HAD A CLIENT, MR. PRYOR (NAME changed), who was diagnosed with stomach cancer. Although the doctors caught it early, he still had a hard time post-surgery. To cheer him up, I had my mother bake him a sweet potato pie (I do not bake) and took it to him. In talking with Mr. Pryor, I asked him how his family was doing. He was candid, telling me that things were not going well between him and his wife. I could tell that he lived alone in the house, as it was "man clean": although not dirty, no dusting or vacuuming had been done for quite some time.

Mr. Pryor was so pleased with the pie that he posted it on his social media stream. His wife saw it and immediately called to check on him. He placed her on speaker, and I chatted with her while he refreshed my tea. During our conversation, Mrs. Pryor said, "Oh my goodness, I hate that you see the house like that. I wish I had had a chance to clean before you came over." I am so glad we were on the phone and not face-to-face because my jaw dropped. I thought to myself, "A WOMAN lives here?!"

Do not get me wrong: I have been in some messy homes before and am aware that there are households where men are the housekeepers, and darn good ones too. The reason I was taken aback was two-fold:

1. The house had not been cleaned for a while and was missing the feminine touches (flowers, air fresheners, decorative pictures, rugs; things that bachelors tend to skip) that we women leave all around to ensure other women know a woman lives here.

2. When Mr. Pryor told me his marriage was on the rocks, I thought he was separated. I thought it odd Mrs. Pryor called to check up on him as a result of his social media post of the pie, but just thought it was a soon-to-be ex being nosy. I had no idea it was a wife checking up on her husband and her house. A house she had clearly forsaken and left as a casualty during their marital war.

When I got home that night, I took a hard look at my own home. I assessed the state of the shelves, the kitchen counter tops, the state of the furniture to ensure it all had the stamp of "woman" on it. But I also took a good look at my husband and assessed his demeanor and bearing to ensure he had the look of a man who was and is cared for. He saw me studying his countenance and asked me what was going on. I explained the day I had, and after he laughed for a full minute and composed himself, he assured me that our home was Woman Approved and that he was quite happy to be Wife Sealed.

But then I began to think. And ponder. And finally, I gave up trying to put a name on it and just laid on in it. I thought about how much hurt must have been in that house. The fear of death and dying that had clearly seized both husband and wife, holding them hostage until . . . until what? Until they gave up all hope – on life, their relationship, their home?

And then I thought about how they could get the hope back. I'm not naïve – I know there were so many other things going on there that I will never know. Possibly an affair, definitely unkind words, maybe even abuse. You just never know. A relationship is like a dance – there are two partners, and only they know the routine. The ransom would be high, but it could be paid. With forgiveness. If I have learned nothing else about life, it is this: We all have choices. We choose to leave and we choose to stay. In this instance, both parties chose to stay. It really does not matter why, but since such decision is an ongoing one (relationships require constant re-commitment), then the parties ought to make it worth their while. Anything else is madness, a true waste of time. Forgiveness allows you to do that and more. I won't say "let it go", but I will say "let God have it". They sound the same but allow me to share the differences.

Letting go means tossing it up in the air. If you've ever thrown something at another person, you know human instinct kicks in so that the person tries to catch it. There are a few exceptions, but generally, people like to step in and save the day. People do not like saying "I don't know" – allowing something to sail past you and hit the ground is the physical equivalent of saying you don't know. It feels wrong, like you let someone down. And most people don't like letting people down – even if they don't like the person who's "tossing". Like a good juggler, if you just "let it go", you're going to stand there and try to catch it when "it" comes down. Your instinct is going to kick in and you're going to see that hard word, that mean action, that rude gesture come sailing at you and you're going to catch it – and hurl it back. Really hard. Unless your AQ is incredibly high (Jesus level), you're going to get caught up in this at least once in your life.

But if you Let God Have It, then you're handing "it" off to the Divine Mind, the Master of the Universe, the Great I Am, to handle it. No matter how hard, how mean, how rude, God's got it. Let Her take it and run with it.

No, it is not going to be easy. At first, there will be a feeling of a void, like something is missing. When that person says something outrageous, you'll initially want to fall back into old behaviors and fire right back at 'em. Don't. Allow silence to rule. When that person does something preposterous, you'll want to rain fury onto her. Don't. Allow reason to stand and walk away. In the "do nothing" void is where you'll find peace. This is where your AQ rises to provide protection and instruction for your good. Peace is allowed to blossom and allows you to take stock of your life and relationship and decide if you want to continue with "this". Because friend, it is a real possibility that you need to be the change you want to see in your world.

Want him to stop cheating? Then stop cheating. Whether that's on your time card at work, on your taxes, or cutting in line at the mall – stop it.

Want her to stop spending so much? Then stop spending. Whether it's time away from home, playing on social media, or reliving the Glory Days – stop it.

In your mind, they are not the same – how can I possibly equate infidelity and butting someone in line? How dare I put posting on IG on the same footing as blowing the mortgage payment on a pair of shoes? Take a breath, break out the Good Book, and take a look at the sins (or separations) noted throughout it. Do you see any equivocating as to which behaviors are worse than others? Or if you're not up to doing the research, look within.

When you have a headache and stomach ache at the same time, does your mind ever say, "Well, my stomach doesn't hurt as bad as my head"? Or does it just say, "I hurt"? We do not take stock in the threshold until someone else asks. Did you hear that? It is not until an external force asks us to check in that we then attempt to rank our pain. But pain has no meter. When we hurt, we just want it to STOP. Period.

Realizing we're in pain is the fastest way to get to the source of it. Realization is your IQ at work. Forgiveness is the fastest and most assured way to stop the pain. Forgiveness is your EQ at work. And peace is the fastest and most assured way to stop the behavior that caused the pain. Peace is your SQ at work. We must have all three quotients working at optimal peak to achieve ultimate AQ.

But what happens when you cannot find peace? What happens when you can't leave a situation or relationship lickety-split? You have bills, you can't just quit your job. You have children, you don't want to break up your home before they go off to college. You love him/her. You don't want to throw away X number of years. What now?

Peace is a state of mind. You get there through prayer and meditation. Pray and meditate. His Holiness, Sri Sri Ravi Shankar, described the difference between prayer and meditation this way: "Prayer is talking to God, and meditation is listening to God." My grandmother, the late First Lady Annie Mae Champion used to say "God gave us two ears and one mouth. We should do twice as much listening as we do talking." So, when we pray and ask the Creator to give us peace, we must sit and be quiet to receive it.

Sit.

Quietly.

There is your peace.

And yet . . . sometimes peace does not be still.

I remember a couple I had the pleasure to meet, Mr. and Mrs. Stephens (names have been changed). They had a home located in the historical Marietta Square. The homes in this area are absolutely incredible. The architecture, landscaping, and Southern charm call to your heart in a way that is incomparable to anything I have seen across the United States. When I entered the house, I was not disappointed to see that the inside was every bit as authentically historical as the outside - beautiful antique furniture, gilded gold mirrors, and floor rugs that probably cost more than some people's homes.

Mr. and Mrs. Stephens were nice people, entrepreneurs who had restored the home and enjoyed living on the Square. During the course of the transaction, I allowed them to guide the conversation, and we chit-chatted about various things, mostly restaurants, vacation spots, and clothing stores that I was not quite yet able to afford, but maybe would be once I really got my practice going.

I remember sighing silently, and thinking to myself, "One day."

When we arrived at the loan application, any feelings of wistfulness or envy evaporated like water on the pavement in 105 degree weather: Mr. and Mrs. Stephens were in debt up to their eyeballs and beyond! There were five pages of credit card accounts that exceed $100,000. Any retail store you can think of appeared on that list and every card carried a balance. This blew my mind because I had never seen - and have never seen since - any loan application where customers had more than two additional pages of debts. And they still had the mortgage on the house, a second mortgage, a line of credit, car notes, and the transaction we were completing was a refinance to pay all of it off and take equity - cash - out of the house for more improvements. This was during the real estate "boom" years, so the home was valued at well over a million dollars, but their debts - all in - were approaching that. This beautiful house, their home, was leveraged to the hilt and there was no room for error.

I was so stunned by all that I had seen that I literally froze. Mrs. Stephens saw my face - I was not as good then as I am now at hiding my emotions - and she began to try to explain. "We have the cash to pay all this off, but we don't want to tie up all our reserves." "We prefer to put the debt against the house so we may use the interest deduction for tax purposes." There were more explanations, but I do not remember them now. The entire time, her husband sat silent, and was still as a stone. I slowly realized that this was the first time he was seeing all this. He had no idea how leveraged they were and how close to disaster should any catastrophe strike.

Do not misunderstand: He knew about the first and second mortgage, as well as the line of credit - he was on the title of the house and the loan, so he had to have signed documents accepting responsibility for payment. And I am sure he knew about some of the credit cards - although most of them were stores where women would normally shop, he very much enjoyed the fruits of the "shopping tree". What I do not think he had ever done was sit down and actually look at all of their accounts compiled in one place, with all debts combined, to understand the extent of how they funded their lifestyle.

We continued the closing, but the warmth that had previously been present was gone. Mr. Stephens shifted his body away from Mrs. Stephens. She noticed it and tried to re-engage him to no avail. In her nervousness in the uncomfortable silence, she began talking - which made it worse. The cash they were taking out of the house to make more home improvements - it was actually to put into their business because things had begun to slow.

When I left that house, I was sad for Mr. and Mrs. Stephens. Although they had been married over 20 years, I was not sure if their marriage was going to survive this blow. As young as I was, even I knew the market would bottom out eventually, and if they did not get a hold of their situation, they would lose everything.

My husband and I had only been married a few years at this point, and the lessons I learned from that encounter all lead me to one thing: We make and break our own peace.

Peace is a state of mind, the highest level of AQ there is. It is the place where we fully embrace our responsibility to be 100% in charge of our state of being, knowing, feeling and doing. When we say "peace, be still," it is the place of calm no matter the storm raging around you: People with better houses, cars, and clothes; children who choose not to follow in your footsteps of faith, business, or sexual orientation; or even diagnoses of illness, stress, or strain.

So how do we cross the threshold of total peace and take the throne of our AQ kingdom? By realizing that there is no scale, no comparison, no measure, nor any grade to achieve. Each person's AQ - YOUR AQ - will differ from every other person's in the world . . . and change constantly throughout your life. But I know you want some way to track your progress; it's only human to do so. We were built to create and constantly "improve" upon what we bring into the world. Here are three ways that I learned to keep my peace without regard to what is going on:

1. LIVE WITHIN MY MEANS.

There is no point trying to keep up with the Joneses (or Stephenses). They are all leveraged to their eyeballs. If they were doing as well as they "put on" to the world, they would not have mortgages, car notes, or excessive credit cards. Living like the Average Joe means having average stress, average worry, and average bills. I can deal with that, particularly since I know that my "average" increases as I increase in success and prosperity.

2. LESS IS MORE.

It is the middle class that keep non-profits and other charities funded in the United States. We understand that it takes donations to keep these wonderful organizations operating in our communities, doing the work that government cannot do nor is suited to do. When you have less bills, you can give more. These deductions on your tax returns are so much more enjoyable to take than others. You know your money is benefiting a cause you care about, you receive a letter or pen thanking you for your donation, and you do not wake up in a cold sweat wondering what you will do if the market comes crashing down on your head.

3. REVIEW FINANCES REGULARLY.

Although I hate it, my husband and I look at our debt list monthly - house, credit cards, and other outstanding debts. We discuss adjustments that need to be made and hold one another accountable for deviations from the plan of action. Sometimes deviations cannot be helped. When I was in the hospital a few years ago, it really hit us hard, so that had to be taken into account. But the point is, we knew what was going on, why it was happening, and planned on how to deal with it - together.

A few months after my meeting with the Stephenses, I drove by that house, just to see if they were still there. There were signs that the Stephenses were no longer in residence: the monogram "S" on the gate was gone, replaced by another letter, the house was for sale and appeared to be in need of repair. I was not surprised, but I was a little sad - I had hoped they would make it through. Debt did them part.

But it did not have to be that way.

Money is the number one reason couples split, partnerships are destroyed, friendships are no longer, and people commit suicide. Actually, that's not correct. The illusion that money is the source of our peace is the number one reason couples split, partnerships are destroyed, friendships have withered away, and people commit suicide.

My father said something to me when I was in high school that I never forgot: "Money is a tool. It is to be used." I did not understand the breathtakingly wise counsel in that simple statement until I was in my late 30's. I had decided to go in a totally different direction with my life – I wrote my first book. I financed everything myself – publishing, marketing, advertising, branding, the works. The money I made from law was used as a tool to fund my new venture. At first, things were grand – people purchased my book, invited me to speak, attended my workshops, and supported my ventures. But then the support slowed steadily until rooms that used to be packed were no longer and instead of recalibrating, I continued doing what I knew – using my law firm to fund my other ventures. The problem with that was when my law firm work began to slow, I did not stop to change course then either – I turned to credit cards. And when the cards were at the limit, I turned to lines of credit. And then finally, when I had exhausted every avenue (financially and mentally), I turned to Who I should have first sought guidance – the Lord.

In my prayer, I remembered what my father told me. "Money is a tool." Tools must be cared for, stored in a safe place, examined from time to time, and sometimes, they too, need to be repaired. I had misused and abused my tools. I had not taken care of them, yet still expected them to care for me. I had run them down into the ground, overworked them, and was laughingly bewildered when they did not perform as they used to.

But there is another part in using tools. No matter how good a tool is on its face, it is the person wielding it that determines its true value. Tools in the hands of a fool make them foolish and dangerous. They break, destroy, and render useless everything they touch. Tools in the hands of a master make them masterFUL. Full of mastery, ready to be employed for the miraculous and amazing. They repair damage, revitalize for extended wear, rejuvenate with new life, and inspire for new purpose.

Because it is the *person* who wields the tool who determines its ultimate value, every day that person – we, us – has a new opportunity to learn to better employ those tools. It is never too late to do better. It is never too late to salvage what was lost. Marilyn Monroe said it best: "Sometimes, things have to fall apart for better things to fall together."

So, I changed my organization around, refocused my attention to the law so I could tighten things back up. In getting my spiritual house in order, I was able to get my financial and mental houses organized, which led to my emotional house coming back together.

Learn from the things that fall apart, but don't allow them to rip you asunder. In other words, don't regret - regroup.

There is a force in this beautiful universe that requires

perfect balance, and that balance is created by all parts and angles - up and down, left and right, in and out, yin and yang. To achieve the balance and maintain the harmony, it requires all parts of the equation, i.e., there must be something on the other side of the "equals" sign. Without both sides of the equation, imbalance and disharmony result. We must stop allowing regret to dictate every area of our lives and guide us to make decisions that are not rooted in wisdom and love. Regret inspires guilt and shame and disgrace, but it should inspire introspective analysis and hope for better in the future. It should require a retooling of how we do things and how we approach life. This process of introspection and retooling is called regrouping.

But regrouping requires help.

When you hire help, such as an assistant, you really need to hire someone who understands your Bubble. Your Bubble is the place that you go that is Total Insanity. It's a place that nobody but someone who loves you will tolerate. You need to hire somebody who understands that your Bubble is just a space in time; it is not indefinite, and it will end.

Many times, we are looking for the best we can get for the least amount that we can pay. I had a conversation not too long ago with a coach who shared something with me that was eye-popping in that it is something we know because we demand it from our clients, but we don't necessarily apply to the people *we* hire. It is better to pay an administrative assistant $40 an hour for two hours of work than to spend eight hours of your valuable time training someone you are paying $15 an hour. This sounds ridiculously simple, but we have all nickel-and-dimed someone thinking we were saving money, only to realize that we have wasted valuable time and self-respect doing so.

But for the sake of illustration, here's the nickel-and-dime version: at $10 an hour you must show the assistant exactly what you need done, going through it with him/her again why what they did the first two times was not right and then finally getting a product that was nowhere near what you had in mind in the first place. If you look at it in terms of your time being money, check this out. If your fees are somewhere north of $500 per hour and you just spent eight hours training someone, *you just spent $4,000 fooling around with someone instead of spending $80 hiring the right person from the beginning.*

You also need to look at this in terms of collateral damage. You are a person with thoughts and feelings. When you work closely with someone, you are going to become more than boss and employee. You are going to care about that person's family and he/she is going to care about yours. You are going to care if he/she had a bad day or if his/her hopes and dreams are being realized, just like that person cares about what's happening with you.

You both understand that you rise and fall together, that it is not just about you, it's about Y'ALL - together. So that means this person you allow into your Bubble needs to be trustworthy, understands confidentiality and keeps it. There needs to be genuine affinity and affection between the two of you. When it's all said and done, money cannot buy that.

And yet I just laid out a case that says that it does - or so it seems. Remember, money is a tool to be used in a responsible manner. When used correctly, it communicates respect and good will. When we spend it wisely and with good intention, whatever we think we lose, we will get back tenfold. God will restore and give you more.

Blessings from the Lessons

1. The only person you are competing against is yourself. The ball you need to keep your eyes on is yours.

2. You are the one you've been waiting for all your life to "save" you, but you must stay focused on what is important - YOU. From there, God can and will create the environment for you to regroup from regret so He may restore everything you think you've lost and give you more than you ever dreamed you could have.

CHAPTER 24

SHOULDER ALL BURDENS WITH FAITH & INTUITIVE WISDOM

A COUPLE OF YEARS BEING ON MY own, I thought I had seen it all. Nope. I had two experiences related to "challenged spouses" that really opened my eyes to how some people take on other people's debt to their own detriment. Both clients were middle-aged women, one Caucasian and the other Hispanic. One raised in the Deep South and the other in Latin America. Yet they handled their challenged spouses the exact same way.

Mrs. Lopez (name has been changed) was an attractive woman with a beautiful cottage-sized home in a nice middle-class community. The home was paid in full, yet she was completing a transaction that would allow her to pay off a car. Previous to this transaction, I had never seen anyone pull equity out of their home to pay off an automobile. Mrs. Lopez's mother was present and spoke rapid Spanish in increasingly angry tones most of my time there. I did not understand every word Mother Lopez said, but I gathered that she did not approve of the transaction.

Mrs. Lopez explained that her mother was angry because the car that was being paid off was that of Mrs. Lopez's husband. He had purchased the car without her knowledge during the housing boom. When the economy went south, so too did his ability to earn income (he was a construction worker) and so he was not able to make the payments. Mrs. Lopez tried to keep up with the payments, but it was just too much to bear with their other responsibilities and their child in college. Hence, the transaction to pay off the car and obtain a low monthly payment that they could afford.

Mr. Lopez was noticeably silent during the entire transaction and left as soon as we were finished. I felt sorry for him, in that I know his pride was bruised by the entire process. However, I felt worse for Mrs. Lopez because she was placed in a situation where she was paying off a car in which she had no interest (when Mr. Lopez bought the car, he put it in his name only), and she was saddling herself with a debt on the one asset she had worked to ensure was free and clear before her daughter went to college to avoid the stress she was now under to make ends meet.

Mrs. Davis (name has been changed) was in a similar bind. After 30 years of marriage, her husband decided he did not wish to be married to her anymore and wanted to begin anew with someone else. When he left, the house they shared was almost paid in full (only two years remained on the mortgage). Although a shock, Mrs. Davis thought that with her impending retirement, she would be able to start her life over again as well. (She was an attractive woman with a great personality.) However, Mr. Davis had amassed a substantial amount of debt in credit cards - over $50,000 - and the cards were in both of the Davis' names. Sadly, Mrs. Davis had no idea these debts were out there until the bill collectors started calling and sending late notices to the house. She figured out then how Mr. Davis was able to finance his affair.

Mrs. Davis' divorce lawyer counseled her to file bankruptcy so the debt would be eliminated. She did not want her credit destroyed by bankruptcy. She refinanced her home, taking out a 20-year mortgage to pay off the credit cards and delaying her retirement. Interestingly, when I met with her to complete the final paperwork, she was not bitter. She sighed a lot but was resigned to things as they were.

Of course, I am on the outside looking in at both of these situations, and I am sure there was more to both of these stories than what I shared above. But even with this limited information, I can reasonably say the following:

1. INDIVIDUAL DEBT AND JOINT DEBT ARE NOT EQUAL.

Both Mrs. Lopez and Mrs. Davis took on their spouses' debts as if they had a hand in accumulating them. And they both wound up singularly liable to pay. That is not right and leads to the second thing.

2. WHILE DEBT IS INCLUDED IN "FOR BETTER OR WORSE", BOTH SPOUSES NEED TO BE PARTNERS IN PAYING OFF AMOUNTS INCURRED.

Mr. Lopez left the room before we finished the transaction because he was embarrassed. I believe that if he had been made a partner in the obligation and repayment, he would have been able to "man up" at the table.

Mr. Davis left his cares behind because he just did not care about the consequences of non-payment (and I believe he had a hunch that Mrs. Davis would react exactly as she did). Mrs. Davis could have and should have stood up for herself, forcing the creditors to pursue the person who ran up the cards. She may have been able to avoid paying the debts by showing that she had no idea the cards had been opened and that she had never used them.

Now, all that being said . . . what now? We've allowed our intellect to play out the "shoulda, woulda, coulda" scenarios, and the field has been cleared, so NOW what are we gonna DO?

1. TAKE RESPONSIBILITY FOR YOUR ACTIONS.

The first thing we've GOTTA do is own our part in things. Dr. Michael Duckett said that "unless and until we own our part in everything that has happened 'to' us, no matter how small, we cannot move on". Every action where we had a choice – no matter how bad our choices were – involved our participation. We must accept and FORGIVE ourselves for those choices. They happened. They have passed. They are in the past. It is time to move on.

But how? It's not like the thoughts just stop coming because we've said the words "I forgive me". How many times have we forgiven others, but the memory of the thing pops up at the weirdest times? How many times have we said to ourselves that we are not going to rehash something only for "something" to rear its ugly head during our "Zen space"? How many times have we been in the positions of Mrs. Lopez and Mrs. Davis where we are being asked to do the seemingly impossible - to move on while we're still in the midst of the consequences of the wrong action?

2. ACT WITH THE FAITH AND INTUITIVE WISDOM OF A CHILD.

My AQ pointed to an unlikely source for the answer as to how we are going to move on: Children. So, I looked at children who forgive their parents every single day for wrong actions that include thoughtless words, harsh punishments, and unreasonable expectations. How do they continue to love Mom and Dad in spite of the mistakes, missteps, and misdirection?

Love. True love. The kind that Jesus had for us. The kind that allows you to see a person's faults and flaws, and yet appreciate the brilliance and wonder that also dwells deep within their soul. The kind that whispers to your soul that although that person has embraced these less-than-optimal behaviors as their current life experience, you do not have to do the same. The kind that allows you to value the time you have enjoyed together, but now realize it is time to move on and do your own thing.

3. MOVE ON AND EMBRACE SOMETHING NEW.

So that's the other thing: We must move on. Continuing to harp, gripe, ruminate, and stew on what was isn't going to get us to what IS. Because right now is what IS – it is the present. "The opportune time is now" is the motto of the Kairos Institute for Progressive Studies founded by

Rev. Rowena Silvera Beck, and perfectly encapsulates this point. There is no other time that matters in our lives but right here and right now. How? Because this is the only time over which we have control. The past is gone, and the present is determined by what is going on today. To seize control of what may be, we must fully confront what IS. Right here, right now.

Once we commit to living in the present, we can devise our plan on how to make NOW pleasurable, truly full of joy. That is the key to unlock our AQ in this experience. For Mrs. Lopez, that encompassed facilitating the healing of her marriage. Her husband made a mistake at a time when many people made the same mistake. He and they believed that the market was not cyclical and that the good times would last forever. He made an expenditure that put their family in a bind once his opportunities for employment dissipated due to the housing crash. And he did the brave thing - he took stock of what IS – at that moment, where he was at that time, being faced with repossession or going to his life partner for help. Mr. Lopez swallowed his pride and together, he and his wife were able to come up with a solution that would help them move forward together.

But what about the fact that the debt was not Mrs. Lopez's? Why should she have to help shoulder this purchase that she didn't make herself? Hmmmm – go back and read the last paragraph. They are life partners.

When a relationship is formed, a new entity is created – a partnership. Under laws of both God and man, a partnership is viewed as a distinct entity from the individuals. It can enter into contract, be sued, start new ventures, grow rich, and file bankruptcy. Partnerships are born, live and die. It's the living that we focus on right now. Mrs. Lopez wanted her partnership to live. Agreeing to allow the partnership to shoulder the burden of the debt made a way for that to happen.

So, what does this mean for Mrs. Davis? How does she live in the NOW when her ex-husband left her hanging with fifty G's of debt probably used to finance an affair with another woman? By owning her choice to pay the debt and preserve her credit. When we choose to fight, even the righteous wars, there is a cost to wage each battle. Mrs. Davis would probably have needed to hire an attorney to battle the credit card companies, dig through the statements for evidence of what was not there (her purchases), obtain independent evidence that she did not benefit at all from those purchases, fight with the credit bureau to update her profile, fight with Mr. Davis about all of the above, and on and on and on. That is a lot of fighting when your soul is already weary, and your heart broken. Author C. Joybell C. says it best: "It's not winning battles that makes you happy, but it's how many times you turned away and chose to look into a better direction. Life is too short to spend it on warring. Fight only the most,

most, most important ones, let the rest go." Mrs. Davis chose to bring to a close the fight, in a way that would allow her to "look into a better direction" as quickly as she could. She wanted to embrace the NOW, truly to be in joy (enjoy) the rest of her life. In this instance, she was not shouldering a burden, but rather alleviating one in a most unconventional, yet effective way.

Your life is yours to live, no matter what other people do or say about or to you. You have the choice in what happens after they do and say whatever. That means that what they have done is in the past, and what you do is in the present. Since you control the present, then you dictate what happens next – the future is truly yours. Release the burdens of others – other people and other times. Your time is NOW. You know this on the most basic level, or you would not continue to get up every day. Furthermore, you know that you are equipped to live life well, your AQ giving you all you need to do so. But as with any other tool, you must USE it. Right now.

Blessings from the Lessons

1. NOW is the only time that matters. In all your relationships, embrace your power now to determine what tomorrow will bring.

2. Love and forgiveness require absolute loyalty to living in the present. The moment you step back

into the past or forward into the future, you cede your ability to be in total control of today.

CHAPTER 25

CHEATING IS STUPID; DON'T BE STUPID. THERE'S NO REASON TO TAKE WHAT IS ALREADY YOURS

STUPID IS DEFINED AS "HAVING OR showing a great lack of intelligence or common sense". I define stupid as the willful act of forgetting who you are and allowing the outside world's warped intelligence to displace your Divine AQ.

I once met a couple of real estate investors who were also married - Mr. and Mrs. Morris (names have been changed). They had a large number of properties, all individually owned, some by Mr. Morris and others by Mrs. Morris. There was one particular property that was owned by Mrs. Morris, but Mr. Morris had done all the leg work on the loan, so he was the one with whom I went over the financials when he arrived in the office. We chatted as we waited for Mrs. Morris, but it quickly became apparent that our small talk was not going to span the duration of her tardiness. We had been waiting 30 minutes, with Mr. Morris sending multiple text and voicemail messages to his wife, with no response.

Finally, Mrs. Morris answered the phone stating she was around the corner. When she finally arrived - 15 minutes later - I knew there was going to be trouble. Her hair was slightly damp and she smelled like she had just gotten out of the shower. She had told her husband on the phone that she had gotten caught in a meeting. And no, she did not work at the gym - Mrs. Morris worked in a corporate office. Sure enough, Mr. Morris noticed the same things I noticed, and immediately started in on her. I stopped him, and steered Mrs. Morris to her seat so we could complete our business. Once done, I quickly vacated the room to give them privacy.

While I waited for World War III to end, I sat wondering . . .

1. Which was Mr. Morris most angered by? The fact that Mrs. Morris was late and almost cost them the deal, that Mrs. Morris was so blatant about what she was doing, or the fact that she was doing something she was not supposed to be doing?

2. What circumstances led to the deterioration of their marriage that caused Mrs. Morris to hold her husband in such low regard to behave in such a manner in front of a complete stranger (me)?

3. If people are going to cheat, why are they stupid when they do it? Children put more effort into cheating on tests than some adults do in having a side item. As glamorous as TV shows make double lives appear, it is more than a notion to maintain (as evidenced by the Morris' situation).

If I've not learned anything else in this life, it is this: there's no point putting on airs. Pretending that everything is grand is a waste of everyone's time (yours included). Not dealing with the things that actually bother you robs you of the opportunity to set things right. But sometimes it is easier to exemplify this simple point by holding up my favorite couple: The Joneses. In 1853, the Jones family built an absolutely incredible mansion on the Hudson River in New York City that is believed to have inspired a building boom so other tycoons of the area could "keep up" with the Joneses. But the Joneses were not focused on what other people had done, they were focused on what could be if they did something right now. (Sound familiar – the time is now.) The Joneses do not care what you have or how you acquired it. They are too busy trying to one up one another and look only to themselves as the mark of excellence. Putting on airs to try to impress others means nothing to them. But sometimes, people have to learn that the hard way. Case in point:

I completed a transaction for an Indian couple who lived in a home valued in the millions. It was palatial in every sense of the word - gilded gates, winding driveway, steep cliff drop off, spiral staircase, marble floors - you get the idea. And the decor was breathtaking - a true artist decorated that home from the rugs to the dishes and the bedding.

I wish the decorator had taken time to work on the character of the people who had hired her . . .

The Braithes (name has been changed) were a power couple. Both had very good jobs earning mid-six-figure incomes. Their children attended a very prestigious private school. They drove luxury cars and wore designer clothes. They were very "highbrow". I admire people who work hard for what they have and think it is good when they buy the things they want. The problem is when they behave stupidly by treating people who complete services for them worse than gum stuck to the bottom of one's shoe.

When I arrived at Braithes' home, they acted as if shaking my hand was begging for leprosy. They conducted personal business as I tried to complete their transaction. The entire time I was there, they behaved as if the transaction was a favor they were doing for the bank, and not one they were doing out of necessity. When it came time to produce a witness for their signatures, they froze. They had forgotten that since they had requested that I come to them, that they would need to provide a witness to the transaction for the notarization. I knew why they were so put out - they did not want the neighbors to know that they were refinancing their home.

I waited patiently for the inevitable to happen, and the Braithes did not disappoint. They began berating me for not bringing a witness as a backup. They tried to bully me into completing the transaction without a witness. They threatened to report me to the lender, saying that I was aloof and unhelpful. Through it all I just repeated the same thing: "Would you like to ask a neighbor or reschedule for another day?" (It was too late in the evening to go to a business to get it taken care of.)

Finally, they relented and called a neighbor. This is the person I will call Mr. Jones. Mr. Jones lived in a similarly majestic home, looked just as successful, and I presume, was married to an equally impressive-on-paper wife. When the Braithes explained what they needed, Mr. Jones replied, "Oh sure, we just did this a month ago."

1. BE YOURSELF, NO NEED TO PUT ON AIRS.

In reviewing the Braithes' loan application, it was plain to see they were living well above their means. Their credit cards all had significant balances, they owed large balances on both cars, they had both a first and second mortgage on the house, and the list goes on. They were working so hard to impress the people around them - the Joneses - that they forgot to just be the Braithes.

While I would not advise allowing people into one's personal affairs if unnecessary, misrepresenting one's position is just not a wise thing to do. You wind up spending more than you have and bringing undue stress into your life to impress people who do not care or who are in the same situation as you are.

2. RESPECT YOURSELF, AND IN SO DOING, YOU SHOW OTHERS HOW TO TREAT YOU.

Stupidity in regard to both of these situations is a form of disrespect because it is a willful disregard for basic courtesy. Oddly enough, even after witnessing the Morris' screaming match and experiencing the Braithes' thinly veiled racism, I believe both couples could still live "realistically happily ever after". Recognition of mutual (shared) interest can overcome just about anything. But there must be honest dialogue in every area of one's life to pull it off. In the case of the Morris', the issue was infidelity. In the instance of the Braithes', it was one of false light. Both examples are that of cheating – being unfaithful to the beautiful divine light inherent in our souls, placed there by the Divine Mind, God. Such cheating robs us of our ultimate goal, which is to achieve brilliant intelligence.

Blessings in the Lesson

1. Cheating is stealing and a total waste of time. You were born with everything you need; it is not necessary to take what is not yours or lie about not taking what is not yours. Dishonest behavior is indicative of low intelligence in each quotient, i.e., it is stupidity. You are not stupid, so don't act like it.

2. There is a saying that goes something like this: "Smart people create, great people steal." Don't strive to be smart or great - these are measures of people who are small minded, focused only on the material realm. Put all your effort into being awe-mazing; they enjoy. Awe-mazing people live in peace and joy, and relish the fruits of their labor.

CONCLUSION

WAKE UP AND STOP SLEEPING WITH THE ENEMY

I BRIEFLY WORKED WITH AN ORGANIZATION that had a serious problem with cleanliness. I'm not talking about a few dust bunnies. I'm talking about a restroom that had not been cleaned professionally in years where black vines and orange spots grew in the commode. I've never seen anything like that in my life. I took it upon myself to clean those restrooms because I had nightmares about something possibly splashing on me.

They finally hired someone to clean, and she did a good job, but then that person found another opportunity. And the employees went back to cleaning the restroom. We were victims sleeping with the enemy and didn't even realize it.

At the same company, there were mites living in the carpet, which had not been cleaned in years and had been in service almost 20 years. Those bugs bit me every day. I put down boric acid - nothing. I vacuumed with my personal Minivac - zip. I emptied an entire can of bug spray- nada. I had become a victim and was sleeping with the enemy.

Years ago Julia Roberts starred in the movie "Sleeping with the Enemy". She was a domestic violence victim who faked her death to escape her husband, but found herself in the unfortunate position of killing him in self-defense when he found her in hiding.

The psyche of domestic violence victims is complex, but not complicated. They are people who are very good at hiding what is really going on. They put a good face on things hoping that things will change. They work hard convincing themselves that the problem must be them and not the person who is torturing them. Because believe that it is torture when someone picks you apart mentally, spiritually, emotionally, and physically.

When we work in environments that attack us, that environment becomes the enemy. When we look at ourselves and we start picking ourselves apart, convincing ourselves that we are the problem, then we become the victim.

I finally got tired and decided to resign. But it was only after I made the decision to leave that I realized that I had decided to leave my abuser. I had decided to stop sleeping with the enemy. But do you know that I still wondered if I was doing the right thing? I didn't have a job lined up. It wasn't until after I decided to leave that I reached out to colleagues for help with my job search. As I was on the phone with one such person, I could feel things crawling on my feet. Someone else might have freaked out, but I saw it as a sign that I was doing the right thing and moved forward. I suspect that it was similar to when a violence victim thinks, "Should I really leave my abuser?" but then winces from the pain of a cracked rib or touches the black eye that she has masterfully covered with makeup.

1. STOP COVERING YOUR BRUISES WITH MAKEUP.

I am not saying go around and brandish wounds with honor, or badger other people you know are in pain to shake up their individual situations - you certainly don't want to make it harder for those who have stayed in their situation. However, lying about the pain, covering it up, and pretending that it's not a problem does not help you or anyone else.

2. TRUST GOD AND MAKE A MOVE.

Get out of the bed and stop sleeping with the enemy. Trust God to help you to find the next thing in your life. Face the things that have led you to believe that you don't deserve anything better. Know that you are the child of the Most High and that He wants the best for you. There is nothing that you could ask Him that He cannot deliver. If you are going to ask for something, ask for the fantastic, the amazing, the impossible, the improbable, the ridiculous. It is major to us, but not to the same God who parted the Red Sea for His people, delivered Africans in America from slavery, and woke you up this morning to be able to read this book. Divine Mind and Great Creator can and will. God then, God now, God forever.

But you have to decide that you are done sleeping. God will not override your desire for your life. Then you have to act. Wake up! Get up and get moving. Don't worry that you don't know where you're going. Just walk, you'll find the path or make one, either way, you have got to get out of there.

3. USE YOUR FEAR TO PROPEL YOU FORWARD, AND DON'T LOOK BACK.

Allow your pain to fortify your courage, fuel your strength, and propel you through fear. It may be dark right now, but darkness has its place in life. It provides quiet solitude for thinking. Darkness provides contrast to light so we appreciate when the dawn comes. And with the dawn comes joy, the breaking of the things that held us down. Embrace the dawn.

If you don't get up, if you continue to sleep with the enemy, you will become the Enemy. How?

You decide what your life will be every day. If you

stay in a situation, in an emotional state, in a place in Mind, it is because you willed it. If you want out - if you want to transition from worm to butterfly - then you must take action and go within. Non-action IS action - it is a decision to continue the status quo. If you are in a job, relationship, or situation that requires you to behave stupidly, act The Fool, stay asleep to endure . . . then it is not worth preserving.

If you preserve it, then you place value on it. If you place value on it, then you will fight to maintain it. If you fight to maintain it, expending the energy to do so leads to the takeover of your mind (IQ). Once it takes over your mindset, it will consume your ever-waking thought and take over your heart (EQ). Once it pervades your heart, it will invade your soul (SQ). And once it has overwhelmed all your quotients, then your entire being is transformed into "it". Your AQ is transmuted into the very thing you've been sleeping with. In this case, the Enemy, better known as FEAR.

The only enemy you must face and overcome is the fear that courses through you. The pain in our lives is a tool to confront that fear, those things that tempt us to take the "easy road" instead of the one that will help us to grow. The discomfort in our lives allows us to remember times of comfort and to be grateful for what we have. The sadness and disappointment in our lives allows us to reflect on times of gladness and joy, and be thankful for them.

FACE IT. SPEAK IT. FORGIVE IT. RELEASE IT.

Face what is going on in your life. Stare it dead in the eyes. Take your time and really take all of "it" in – the good, bad, and ugly. Acknowledge what is and be honest about what you feel.

Speak aloud what has transpired. Articulate clearly and without reservation the ins and outs, ups and downs, of the whole shebang. Scream, cry, curse, rant, rave, sigh, bark – do whatever you have to do to get it all out!

Forgive the Who, What, When, Where and How "it" all went down. You will not forget it, but you will forgive it. "For" as in "to be in support of or in favor of"; and "give" as in "the capacity to bend or alter in shape under pressure". Be in support of your ability to alter the shape of your life. Decide to transform your thoughts, and therefore your circumstances, in regard to "it" so that only the lesson and blessing remain.

Release the darkness and confusion, and leave them behind. Embrace the fullness of All That Is and know that you are always (and in all ways) surrounded by love and support. Your entire life is for you – to love, be in love, enjoy, be in joy, experience, be experienced, grow, and be in growth. Any person, place, thing, or circumstance that is not in alignment with your Supreme Performance has got to GO.

How and when you decide to face it, speak it, forgive

it, and leave it is up to you. The process is cyclical and some facets of it may require more than one time around the sun. Take the journey and enjoy it.

Transform your life pain into your ultimate gain. Embrace the pain and watch the blessings reign.

The End.

ABOUT THE AUTHOR

LYNITA MITCHELL-BLACKWELL IS A Supreme Performance Personal and Professional Development Coach whose clients experience maximum Life ROI by leveraging her skills and expertise as an Attorney, CPA, Certified Christian Life Coach and Emotional Intelligence Practitioner, and New Thought Christian Practitioner (minister).

With every professional accomplishment and "win", there was an equal and corresponding challenge and "loss" that included a brutal battle with endometriosis, struggles with self-esteem and body-image, and career changes that created terrifying fork-in-the-road decisions. Lynita now uses these experiences to help others live Supreme Performance lives through her system of Aggregate Intelligence development. Resources include books, personal and professional development coaching, webinars and seminars, and transformational keynotes.

Lynita has founded and led several businesses that include an eponymous law firm through which she has been recognized as a Top 100 Lawyer in Georgia; an accounting firm; an award-winning media company that published five magazines, two of which were voted as ATL's Hottest; publishing company that published 7 bestselling authors; and leadership training and development non-profit for which she received the US President's Council on Service & Civic Participation Lifetime Achievement Award. Lynita has been recognized by *Black Enterprise Magazine* as "BE NEXT Under 35" Young & Bold Business Leader, as an Outstanding Georgia Citizen by the Secretary of State, and with the Yellow Rose Community Service Leader Award by the Georgia Women's Legislative Caucus.

To learn more about Lynita or to invite her into your private, public or civic organization, visit www.LynitaMitchellBlackwell.com, and download the Leading Through Living app in the Google Play and Apple App Store.

Made in the USA
Columbia, SC
18 February 2021